outside the narrative

Tom Leonard: Previous Publications

Six Glasgow Poems, Other People Publications, Glasgow 1969
A Priest Came on at Merkland Street, Midnight Press, Glasgow 1970
Poems, E. & T. O'Brien, Dublin 1973
Bunnit Husslin, Third Eye Centre, Glasgow 1975
Three Glasgow Writers (with Alex Hamilton and James Kelman), Molendinar Press, Glasgow 1976
My Name is Tom (soundpoem score), Good Elf Press, London 1978
If Only Bunty Was Here (radio play), Print Studio Press, Glasgow 1979
Ghostie Men, Galloping Dog Press, Newcastle 1980
Satires and Profanities, (Political Revue Pieces), Scottish Trades Union Congress, Glasgow 1984
Intimate Voices: Selected Work 1965-83, Galloping Dog Press, Newcastle upon Tyne 1984; republished Vintage, London 1995, etruscan books 2003
Situations Theoretical and Contemporary, Galloping Dog Press, Newcastle, 1986
Two Members' Monologues and *A Handy Form for Artists for Use in Connection with the City of Culture*, The Edward Polin Press, Glasgow 1990
nora's place, Galloping Dog Press, Newcastle 1990
On the Mass Bombing of Iraq and Kuwait, commonly known as The Gulf War with *Leonard's Shorter Catechism*, AK Press, Stirling 1991
Places of the Mind: The Life and Work of James Thomson (B.V.), Cape, London 1993
A Letter in Reply to a Request for a poem for a Poems for Bosnia *anthology, 'in which* The Independent *has an interest'*, Infolio, Cambridge 1994
Reports from the Present, Cape, London 1995
Etruscan Reader V, (with Tom Raworth, Bill Griffiths), etruscan books, Devon 1997
access to the silence: Poems and Posters 1984-2004, etruscan books, Devon 2004
inside looking in, Survivors Press, Glasgow, 2004
Being a Human Being, Object Permanence, Glasgow 2006

As editor:
Radical Renfrew: Poetry from the French Revolution to the First World War, Polygon, Edinburgh, 1990

outside the narrative

Poems 1965 • 2009

Tom Leonard

etruscan books   Word Power Books

2011

Jointly published by etruscan books and Word Power Books
 Second printing 2011

etruscan books
Elm House
Stowe Lane
Exbourne
West Devonshire EX20 3RY
<atetruscan@aol.com>
www.e-truscan.co.uk

Word Power Books
43-45 West Nicolson Street
Edinburgh EH8 9DB
Scotland
<www.word-power.co.uk>

ISBN: 0-9566283-3-8
978-0-9566283-3-6

The publication of outside the narrative was in part made possible by a grant from the Arts Council, England.

etruscan books are distributed by S.P.D., 1341 7th Street, Berkeley CA, 94710, USA, and are available from Collected Works, Level One, Nicholas Building, 37 Swanston Street, Melbourne 3000, Australia.
<collectedworks@mailcity.com>

Typeset by Robert W. Palmer at Tuff Talk Press, Shirehampton
<robert_w_palmer@lineone.net>

Printed and bound by Aldgate Press, London

http://www.tomleonard.co.uk website

To
the smallpress poet-publishers

Tom McGrath	Other People, Midnight Press
Thomas O'Brien	E & T O'Brien
Lawrence Upton	Good Elf Press
Tom Raworth	Infolio
Gerry Loose	Survivors Press
Peter Manson	Object Permanence

Pete Hodgkiss Galloping Dog Press

Nicholas Johnson etruscan books
with typesetter Robert Palmer ("Skip")

CONTENTS

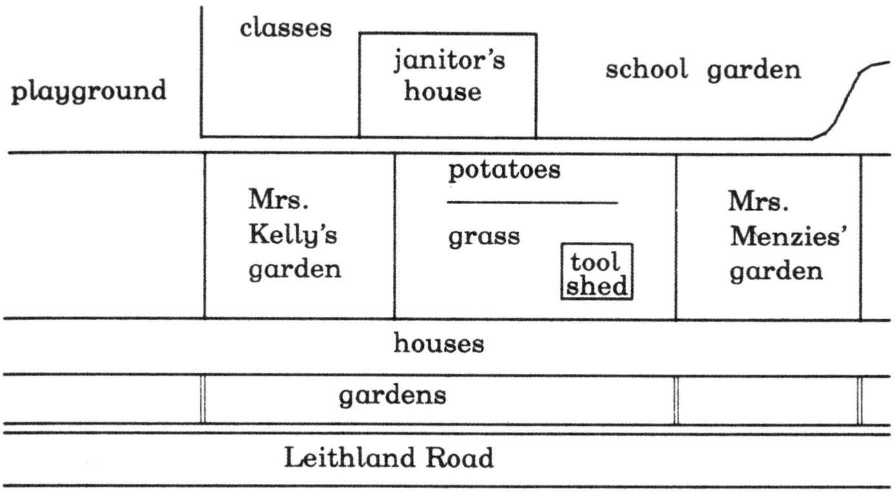

sitting in the garden
behind the toolshed
reading Thomas Mann
Beethoven on the transistor
a blackbird in the potato patch
the grass full of daisies
sweat on my forehead
an insect on my arm
kids in the playground
Mrs. Kelly's fence

the roar of a lawnmower
pause
the roar of a lawnmower
pause
the roar of a lawnmower

Six Glasgow Poems

(1) THE GOOD THIEF

heh jimmy
yawright ih
stull wayiz urryi
ih

heh jimmy
ma right insane yirra pape
ma right insane yirwanny us jimmy
see it nyir eyes
wanny uz

heh

heh jimmy
lookslik wirgonny miss thi gemm
gonny miss thi GEMM jimmy
nearly three a cloke thinoo

dork init
good jobe theyve gote thi lights

(2) SIMPLE SIMON

thurteen bluddy years wi thim ih
no even a day aff
jiss gee im thi fuckin heave
weeks noatiss nur nuthin
gee im thi heave
thats aw

ahll tellyi sun
see if ah wiz Scot Symon
ahd tell thim wherrty stuff thir team
thi hole fuckin lota thim
thats right

a bluddy skandal thats whit it iz
a bluddy skandal

sicken yi

(3) COLD, ISN'T IT

wirraw init thigithir missyz
geezyir kross

(4) A SCREAM

yi mist yirsell so yi did
we aw skiptwirr ferz njumptaffit thi lights
YIZIR AW PINE THEY FERZ THIMORRA
o it wizza scream
thaht big shite wiz dayniz nut

tellnyi jean
we wirraw shoutn backit im
rrose shoutit shi widny puhllit furra penshin
o yi shooda seeniz face
hi didny no wherrty look

thing iz tay
thirz nay skool thimorra
thi daft kunt wullny even getiz bluddy ferz

(5) THE MIRACLE OF THE BURD AND THE FISHES

ach sun
jiss keepyir chin up
dizny day gonabootlika hawf shut knife
inaw jiss cozzy a burd

luvur day yi
ach well
gee it a wee while sun
thirz a loat merr fish in thi sea

(6) GOOD STYLE

helluva hard tay read theez init
stull
if yi canny unnirston thim jiss clear aff then
gawn
get tay fuck ootma road

ahmaz goodiz thi lota yiz so ah um
ah no whit ahm dayn
tellnyi
jiss try enny a yir fly patir wi me
stick thi bootnyi good style
so ah wull

The Voyeur

what's your favourite word dearie
is it wee
I hope it's wee
wee's such a nice wee word
like a wee hairy dog
with two wee eyes
such a nice wee word to play with dearie
you can say it quickly
with a wee smile
and a wee glance to the side
or you can say it slowly dearie
with your mouth a wee bit open
and a wee sigh dearie
a wee sigh
put your wee head on my shoulder dearie
oh my
a great wee word
and Scottish
it makes you proud

Dripping with Nostalgia

while the judges
in the Snottery Weans Competition
were still licking clean
the candidates' upper lips

the "Dear Aul' Glesca" Poetry Prize
for the most heartwarming evocation
of communal poverty
was presented to the author of

"The Day the Dug ate ma Ration Book"

Non Sum Qualis Eram Bonae Sub Regno Cynarae

between the kisses
and the wine

and the wee heavies
and the newcastle browns
and the special brews
and the half bottles of grouse
and the merrydown cider
and the bell's
and the whyte & mackay's
and the dewar's
and the glen grant's
and the glen moranje's
and the odd bottle of old england
and the nembies
and the acid
and the moroccan grass

I have been faithful to thee, Cynara!
in my fashion

don’t tell wordsworth

she dwelt among the untrodden ways
and went her messages by helicopter

Four of the Belt

Jenkins, all too clearly it is time
for some ritual physical humiliation;
and if you cry, boy, you will prove
what I suspect – you are not a man.

As they say, Jenkins, this hurts me
more than it hurts you. But I show you
I am a man, by doing this, to you.

When you are a man, Jenkins, you may hear
that physical humiliation and ritual
are concerned with strange adult matters
– like rape, or masochistic fantasies.

You will not accept such stories.
Rather, you will recall with pride,
perhaps even affection, that day when I,
Mr. Johnstone, summoned you before me,
and gave you four of the belt

like this. And this. And this. And this.

The Psychopath

This time of mourning, cynical laughter,
Rather untragic sunshine, and the
Grotesque church, filled to the aisles
With women, quietly weeping: a coffin,
Light, diminutive – a nation filled with
Posthumous love for the small boy,
Strangled for the newspapers.

The field lay quiet under the summer heat,
No longer involved with time and charted
Place: the people were gone – no customary
Litter, even, to suggest their memory.

A scene painted, perhaps, by a nostalgic
Artist, of limited talent: with the trees
Obediently still, and the grass, and the sky,
And two figures – I, and a boy of twelve,
Who thought I knew his uncle.

The Appetite

That conversation was a tread,
a trampoline. “Words are absurd”,
it said, and our eyes played
at not being on it, laughing.

We sat facing each other, eating
as if
we sat facing each other, eating.

Storm Damage

There is a stain on the ceiling above the bed.
Rainwater. A relic of last year's storm.
It is roughly circular. Darkest at the centre.
The perimeter is not clearly defined.

Eclipse. Your body moves on mine.
Your face looks down on me.
The lips are smiling. The stain
Becomes a halo round your head.

My mind goes back twelve years.
I am a child again, lying in the grass,
Staring into the sky. Eclipse.

You ask me what I'm thinking.

A PRIEST
CAME ON AT
MERKLAND STREET
HILLHEAD
KELVINBRIDGE
SAINT GEORGE'S CROSS
COWCADDENS
BUCHANAN STREET
SAINT ENOCH
BRIDGE STREET
WEST STREET
SHIELDS ROAD
KINNING PARK
CESSNOCK
COPLAND ROAD
GOVAN CROSS
MERKLAND STREET
PARTICK CROSS

A
very thoughtful poem,
being a canonical penance
for sufferers of psychosomatic asthma.

oh no
holy buttons
sad but dignified
and sitting straight across from me
a troubled soul
my son
christ
a bit of Mahler's Seventh might drown him
dah dum, da dum dah dee,
dah dah dah DAH da dah
da DAH, dah DEE da da da
DUM DUM dah dee
hello there
when I'm dead
when I think I'm dead
and I'm in my box
and it's all dark
and I'm wondering where the air's coming from
I'll see this curtain
and it will move to the side
and your great horrible leering face
how many times my son
and how long ago was this
bless me father for I am tinned
christ

maybe he's saying hail mary's
maybe he's praying for all the souls in purgatory
and really sincere
the nicest man in the world
he really loves people
hello father
I'm going to give you a smile
I'm going to give you the nicest smile in the world
it will be real love
there will be absolutely no sex
we will both be five years old
and we'll go to school together
play at weekends together
and you'll climb inside my box
laughing
lying together in the dark
innocent as hell
like after lights out in a school dormitory
cosy but exciting
and maybe God will look round the curtain
hello there
softly as God would say it
and we'll all go away together
away through his door
for ever
amen
I always spoil it
but maybe you'd spoil it yourself
maybe you wouldn't be five years old at all
and you'd climb inside my box
a troubled soul
my son
with a keyhole in your back
wind me up in the morning

and a button under your right arm
how many times my son
and a button under your left arm
how long ago was this
and a button in the back of your head
press to bless
and a tape recorder between your ears
from henceforth ye shall catch men
from henceforth ye shall catch men
from henceforth ye shall catch men
dah dum, da dum dah dee,
oh no
you won't catch me
maybe I'll be really dead
as dead as everyone else who has died
just lying in a box
a box that somebody's made
a box for dead people
and I won't even know
christ
my name is Ozymandias
king of Leithland Road
Pollok
Glasgow SW3
and all the worrying
all the wanting to be five years old
imagine
the lone and level
far away
amen
only it's not the lone and level at all
for there's the Lansdowne Clinic for Functional Nervous
  Disorders

and the Southern General Hospital Department of
Psychological Medicine
and Leverndale formerly known as Hawkhead
Mental Asylum
I could write to a psychiatrist
a cry from the heart
dear sir
my name is Ozymandias
king of Leithland Road
and then there's the box
yours sincerely
maybe faithfully would be better
you know who
ps
I always spoil it
pps
I am awful lonely
ppps
I don't know what people are for
oh no
maybe I think about the box too much
maybe nobody else thinks about the box at all
at least not for long
not more than five minutes a day
or maybe ten minutes at the weekend
and that's all they need
they usually think about something else
they think about something else for hours on end
maybe I should do the same
I could draw up a plan
I could draw up a list of things to think about
everything but the box
and I'd think about them all day

I wouldn't think about the box at all
and then I'd go away home at night
and I'd have my tea
oxtail soup
a plate of potatoes and mince
two slices of toasted cheese
and a cup of tea
that would be fine
that would be very nice indeed
and then I'd go upstairs to my room
and I'd sit down at the table
and I'd write it out twenty times
I am going to die
imagine
maybe I'd get up in the morning
with a big smile
and I'd throw open the bedroom windows
hello there
I have accepted the box
I have accepted that I am going to die
oh no
maybe it wouldn't work at all
maybe I would just stay the same way for years
just thinking about something else all day
not thinking about the box at all
and then just going away home at night
just having my tea
just a cup of tea
maybe a bun
sad as hell
wanting to be five years old
christ

maybe I would tear up my plan
maybe I would tear up my list of things to think about
and I'd just go upstairs to my room
away through my door
for ever
with no button under my right arm
I am going to die
and no button under my left arm
I am going to die
and no button in the back of my head
I am going to die
but a tape recorder between my ears
I am going to die
I am going to die
I am going to die
dear Ozymandias
there is nothing wrong with you at all
my name is Ozymandias two
correction
my name is Ozymandias too
we are all in the box toogether
correction
we are all in the box twogether
correction
we are all in the box together
only indifferent ones
sorry
only in different ones
yours sincerely
you know whoo
correction
you know whwo
correction

you know who
correction
"You Know Who"
imagine
maybe there's nothing wrong with me at all
maybe I'm just the same as everyone else who has lived
and I'll just put on a smile at the box
I'll just put on the nicest smile in the world
and a bit of Mahler's Seventh might drown it
dah dum, da dum dah dee,
dah dah dah DAH da dee
correction
da da da DAH da da
correction
dah dah dah DAH da dah
tick tock
tick
oh no
tick tock
tick
hello there
tick tock
tick
hello there everybody
tick tock
tick

tick tock
tick

tick tock
tick

brackets watch him he has a stoop and funny eyes

AN

OXFORD

DICTIONARY

OF

AN

ENGLISH

LANGUAGE

Poetry

the pee as in pulchritude,
oh pronounced ough
as in bough

the ee rather poised
(pronounced ih as in wit)
then a languid high tea ...

pause: then the coda –
ray pronounced rih
with the left eyebrow raised
– what a gracious bouquet!

Poetry.
Poughit. rih.

That was my education
– and nothing to do with me.

Jist ti Let Yi No
(from the American of Carlos Williams)

ahv drank
thi speshlz
that wurrin
thi frij

n thit
yiwurr probbli
hodn back
furthi pahrti

awright
they wur great
thaht stroang
thaht cawld

Tea Time

ahm thaht depehhhhndint
hingoanti ma vowwwwulz
hingoanti ma maaaammi

howz thi time

ma manz thaht diffffrint
awfa shoart vowwwwulz
hizthaht indipehhhhndint

ahl bettr away

Paroakial

thahts no whurrits aht
thahts no cool man
jiss paroakial

aw theez sporran heads
tahty scoan vibes
thi haggis trip

bad buzz man
dead seen

goahty learna new langwij
sumhm ihnturnashnl
Noah Glasgow hangup
bunnit husslin

gitinty elektroniks man
really blow yir mine
real good blast
no whuhta mean

mawn
turn yirself awn

A Summer's Day

yir eyes ur
eh
a mean yir

pirrit this wey
ah a thingk yir
byewtifl like ehm

fact
fact a thingk yir
ach a luvyi thahts

thahts
jist thi wey it iz like
thahts ehm
aw ther iz ti say

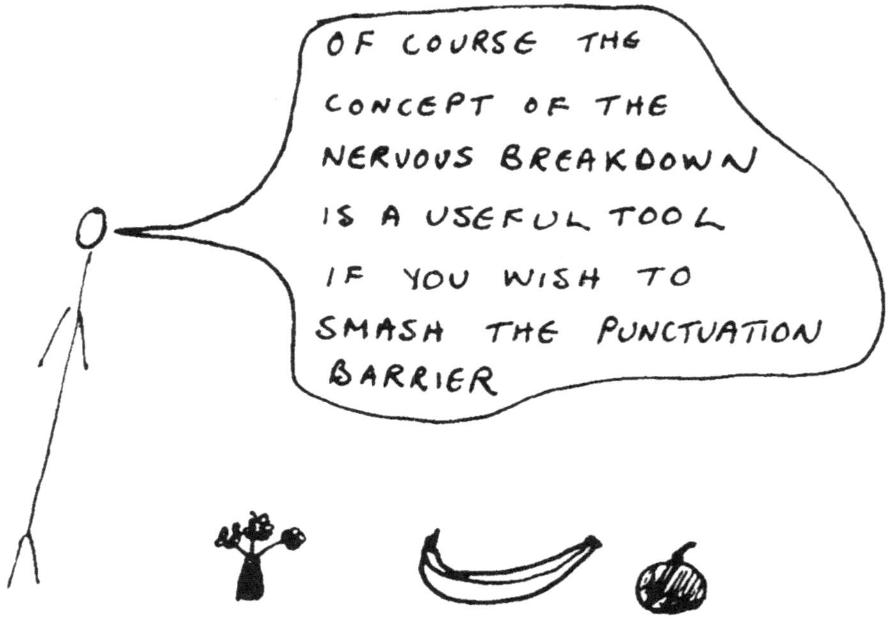

Still Life with Creative Writing Teacher

Yon Night

yonwuz sum night
thi Leeds gemmit Hamdin
a hunnirn thurty four thousan
aw singin
yilnivir wok alone

wee burdnma wurk then
nutsnur a wuz
but she wuzny intristid
yi no thi wey

well there wuzza stonnin
ana wuz thaht happy
ana wuz thaht fed up
hoffa mi wuz greetnaboot Celtic
anhoffa mi wuz greetnaboot hur

big wain thata wuz
a kin laffitit noo

Feed Ma Lamz

Amyir gaffirz Gaffir. Hark.

> nay fornirz ur communists
> nay langwij
> nay lip
> nay laffn ina sunday
> nay g.b.h. (septina wawr)
> nay nooky huntn
> nay tea-leaven
> nay chanty rasslin
> nay nooky huntn nix doar
> nur kuvitn their ox

Oaky doaky. Stick way it
– rahl burn thi lohta yiz.

The Qualification

wurk aw yir life
nuthnty show
pit oanthi nyuze
same awl drivl

yoonyin bashn
wurkir bashn
lord this
sir soan soa thaht

shood hearma boay
sayzwi need gunz
an armd revalooshn
nuthn else wurks

awright fur him thoa
uppit thi yooni
tok aw yi like therr
thats whit its fur

The Dropout

scrimpt nscraipt furryi
urryi grateful
no wan bit

speylt useless yi urr
twistid izza coarkscrew
cawz rowz inan empty hooss

yir fathir nivirid yoor chance
pick n choozyir joab
a steady pey

well jiss take a lookit yirsell
naithur wurk nur wahnt
aw aye

yir clivir
damm clivir
but yi huvny a clue whutyir dayn

Fireworks

up cumzthi wee man
beats three men
slingzowra crackir

an Lennux
aw yi wahntia seenim
coolizza queue cumbir

bump

rightnthi riggin
poastij stamp
a rockit

that wuzzit
that wuzthi end

finisht

MAKARS' SOCIETY

GRAN' MEETIN'
THE NICHT
TAE DECIDE THE SPELLIN'
O' THIS POSTER.

ADMISSION : THRITTY PEE
(A HEID)

Crack

cuts inty thi box
croass cumzthi centre hoff
a right big animull

crack

doon goes Dalgleesh
ref waves play on
nay penahlti

so McNeill complainzty im
oot cumzthi book

tipicl
wan mair upfurthi luj

Pfff

guhta light

fuck me
skirt upty here
thaht size

tah

jeezus crise tam
wee firm arss yi no
whuht kinyi day

pffff

middla Sucky Hall Street
fuckin big hard dawn
nearly shot ma load

pffff

its no right thaht naw
naw its no right thaht

pffff

bluddy blaizir oanur tay
stullit fuckin skool

Moral Philosophy

whiji *mean* whiji mean

lissn
noo lissnty mi toknty yi
right

h hawd oan
whair wuzza
naw

aye
whitsiz name
him way thi
yi no yon

here
here yoo
yir no eevn lissnin
name a god

a doant no

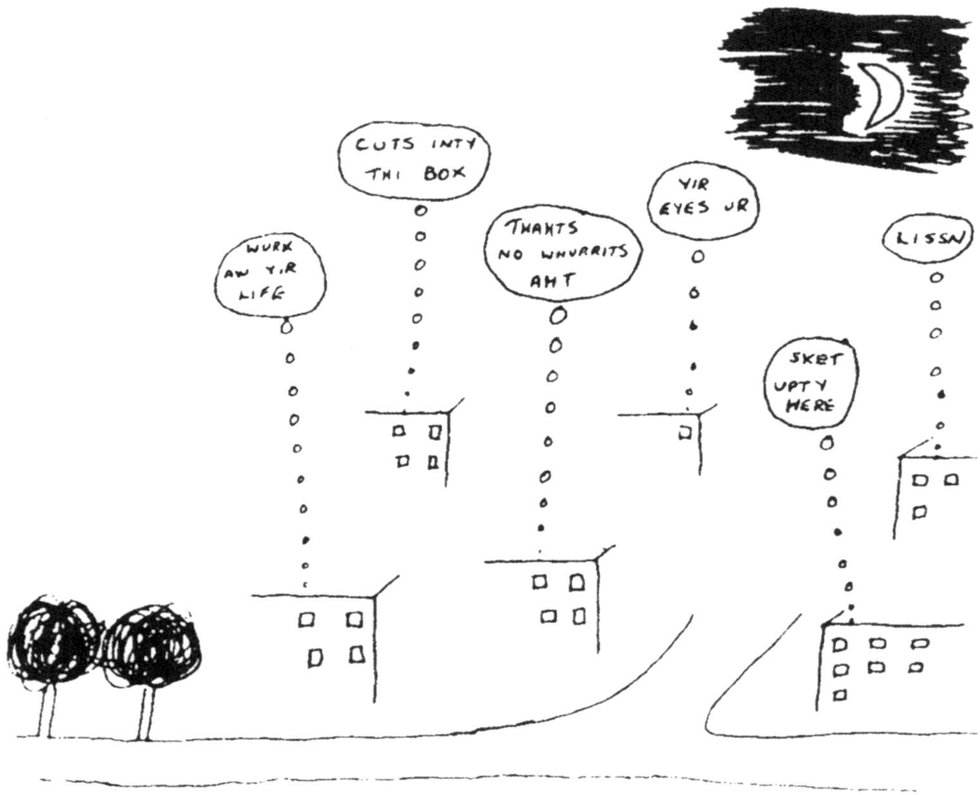
WURK AW YIR LIFE
CUTS INTY THI BOX
THAHTS NO WHURRITS AHT
YIR EYES UR
SKET UPTY HERE
LISSN

My Parents' Living-Room at Christmas

In a converted Dinky garage beside the wireless,
The three wise kings, who have travelled
All the way from Burns & Oates in Buchanan Street,
Peer at the infant under a torch-bulb.

The garage is covered with cotton wool.
Wired to the roof, an angel holds out the message:
"Peace on earth. Goodwill to men."

Fathers and Sons

I remember being ashamed of my father
when he whispered the words out loud
reading the newspaper.

"Don't you find
the use of phonetic urban dialect
rather constrictive?"
asks a member of the audience.

The poetry reading is over.
I will go home to my children.

Placenta

Good-bye to that good woman
who fed you life through a cord
and pushed you into the world:

leave go the rope –
let the weight of her body
leave you. Let the grave

be stitched up. In nine months
the scar will be invisible.

The Rainbow Of

the night wind no   the

        sense of; the sense   of

the night wind   no

the the the the the the the the the the the the
the the the the the the the the the the the the
the the the the the the the the the the the the
the the the the the the the the the the the the
the the the the the the the the the the the the

the night wind no   the

              sense of; the sense   of

the sense of this
the sense of this
the sense of this
the sense of this
the sense of this
the sense of this
the sense of this
the sense of this
the sense of this
the sense of this
the sense of this
the sense of this
the sense of this
the sense of this
the sense of this
the sense of this
the sense of this
the sense of this
the sense of this
the sense of this
the sense of this

the red of the orange of the yellow of the green of
the blue of the indigo of the violet

the orange of the yellow of the green of the blue of
the indigo of the violet of the red

the yellow of the green of the blue of the indigo of
the violet of the red of the orange

the green of the blue of the indigo of the violet of
the red of the orange of the yellow

the blue of the indigo of the violet of the red of
the orange of the yellow of the green

the indigo of the violet of the red of the orange of
the yellow of the green of the blue

the violet of the red of the orange of the yellow of
the green of the blue of the indigo

this the of sense
the this of sense
this the of sense
the this of sense
this the of sense
the this of sense
this the of sense
the this of sense
this the of sense
the this of sense
this the of sense
the this of sense
this the of sense
the this of sense

the day calm yes   the
      sense of; the sense   of

the day calm   yes

this this this this this this this this this this
this this this this this this this this this this
this this this this this this this this this this
this this this this this this this this this this
this this this this this this this this this this

the day calm yes   the
       sense of; the sense   of

breathe deep, and regular with it

if yiv nuthin ti say lets
not talk about not
sayin it if

yiv nuthin ti talk
about lets not
analyse yir

not beein able ti
talk about yir
not beein able ti

say if yiv nuthin
ti analyse talkin
about if lets

say not talkin about
not analysin nuthin
is if not not

talking about is
sayin lets analyse
about nuthin if

through analysin not
not talkin is
sayin not everything

Rosebud

ah mine oh ah mine
whin ah wuzza wee boay

doonit saltcoats
doonit ma aunties

nah shatma drawrz
n flashd ma wullie
booboob be boob

nma aunties n uncles
wur black affruntit

tut tut they sayz
a dampt disgrace

100 Differences Between Poetry and Prose

poetry stops before the end of the margin
you can talk about prose without mentioning school
you don't read poetry to get from Glasgow to Saltcoats without noticing

John Menzies doesn't stock poetry
whoever heard of war & peace having the line as a unit of semantic yield
you can call a poem what you want and say its poetic licence

poetry is the subliminal history of linguistic shape
ahem
poetry has four wheels, two wings and a pair of false teeth

poetry is the heart and the brain divided by the lungs
poetry is the world's oldest cock and fanny story

you don't get prose in anapaestic dimeters
nobody publishes their first slim volume of prose
aristotle never wrote The Proses

if you dribble past five defenders, it isn't called sheer prose
poets are the unacknowledged thingwaybobs

poetry is quintessentially contrapuntal
the square root of poetry is an ever-evolving quark
whenever Vergil looked in the mirror, he beheld an epic Latin poet

poetry is all the juicy bits in the juiciest order
poetry is jellied religion
pascal: if your labourers complain too much, try taking them to a poetry reading

prose goes scchhpludd
prose goes scchhpludd scchhpludd clomp clomp clomp
are you sitting comfortably

then I'll end

The Evidence
(Sheriff Court: Glasgow, April 1995)

I gave chase
to the appellant
with his bucket and billposters

and he fell, my lord,
on the point of my apprehending
him. At which point

I too fell down
- we had come to a grassy slope -
and coming to, I found

the appellant lying
with a bloodied face
on the adjacent path.

My colleague constable lindsay
who had herself fallen down
in the chase, saw nothing of this:

but she arrived in time to find
myself and the appellant
lying some feet apart.

That witness was lying
who said I stood over Mr Anwar
and kicked him where he lay;

nor did I tell the appellant:
"This is what happens
to black boys with big mouths".

The truth is that I felt sorry for him,
so I called an ambulance,
which I boarded with my colleague

and therein charged the appellant
under the Environment Protection Act, Scotland,
with the illegal posting of bills.

proem

who are we, trapped in our ways
                        of dying towards the fact
of only once having been, together

or separate in our own being
            but never wholly separate, only a part
of the time we live in, and with others occupy

(1)

who wants to be free
who has need of air

who is changing

who has a different definition
who has no definition

instance
(the right)

who wants to find out what it is
who wants to go forward

who wants to

(2)

your eyes

the iris grey or is it green
the blue iris

we both love
safely, using the word

and the freschia
with the smell of freschia

filling the room
coming home,
surprised

that place we share

An Ageing Writer

The early angular anger
is now
an avuncular geniality;

the early humour,
- an earnestness of poise.

It's difficult to stay angry
on a full belly;

- difficult to stay funny
on a bitterly swallowed pill.

The Performance

A concert-hall. The auditorium dimmed, the platform lit. An orchestra is playing the closing bars of, say, Brahms' First Symphony. Applause. The conductor bows. The auditorium is lit. Close-up: a face with a look of contentment.

A chapel, lit throughout. The priest is celebrating the closing moments of the Mass for, say, the Fourteenth Sunday after Pentecost. He is heard to say, "The Mass is ended. Go forth in peace." The congregation replies, "Thanks be to God." Close-up: a face, with a look of contentment.

A room. A bed. A man and a woman. Intercourse. Increasing light – say dawn. Close-up: a face, with a look of contentment.

Man: "Bastard!"
Woman: "Stop it!"

Lash.

Pause for five seconds.

Man: "Bastard!"
Woman: "Stop it!"

Lash.

Pause for five seconds.

Man: "Bastard!"
Woman: "Stop it!"

Lash.

Pause for five seconds.

A concert-hall, lit throughout. An orchestra tuning-up. Applause. The leader of the orchestra enters, followed by the conductor. The auditorium is dimmed. Silence. The orchestra begins to play Brahms' First Symphony.

A chapel, lit throughout. The congregation is kneeling. The congregation stands. Two altar boys enter, followed by the priest. The congregation kneels. The priest begins to celebrate the Mass for the Fourteenth Sunday after Pentecost.

A room. A bed. A man and a woman. Intercourse. Night-fall.

Woman: “Bastard!”
Man: “Stop it!”

Lash.

Pause for five seconds.

Woman: “Bastard!”
Man: “Stop it!”

Lash.

Pause for five seconds.

Woman: “Bastard!”
Man: “Stop it!”

Lash.

Pause for five seconds.

A chapel. A bed. The chapel is dimmed, the bed is lit. An altar boy is tuning-up two priests. Intercourse. The orchestra begins to celebrate the Mass for the Fourteenth Sunday after Pentecost. Increasing light – say dawn.

A room, lit throughout. The leader of the orchestra, followed by a woman.

Priest: “Bastard!”
Congregation: “Stop it!”

Silence. Brahms’ First Symphony. Go forth in peace.

Close-up: a face, with a look of contentment. The face is dimmed, the contentment is lit. Night-fall.

Conductor: “Brahms’ First Symphony!”
Orchestra: “Applause!”

Lash.

Pause for five seconds.

Priest: “The Mass is ended. Go forth in peace.”
Congregation: “Thanks be to God!”

Lash.

Pause for five seconds.

Man: “Lash”
Woman: “Pause for five seconds.”

Lash.

Pause for five seconds.

epitaph

you forced open the door
for the trapped

who broke through
shouting

out of the way
half-opener of doors

. in the beginning was the word .
in thi beginning was the wurd
in thi beginnin was the wurd
in thi biginnin was the wurd
in thi biginnin wuz the wurd
n thi biginnin wuz thi wurd
nthi biginnin wuzthi wurd
nthibiginnin wuzthiwurd
nthibiginninwuzthiwurd
. in the beginning was the sound .

from **Unrelated Incidents**

(2)

ifyi stull
huvny
wurkt oot
thi diff-
rince tween
yir eyes
n
yir ears;
– geez peace,
pal!
fyi stull
huvny
thoata lang-
wij izza
sound-system;
fyi huvny
hudda thingk
aboot thi dif-
frince tween
sound
n object n
symbol; well,
ma innocent
wee
friend – iz

god said ti
adam:

a doant kerr
fyi caw it
an apple
ur
an aippl -
jist leeit
alane!

(3)

this is thi
six a clock
news thi
man said n
thi reason
a talk wia
BBC accent
iz coz yi
widny wahnt
mi ti talk
aboot thi
trooth wia
voice lik
wanna yoo
scruff. if
a toktaboot
thi trooth

lik wanna yoo
scruff yi
widny thingk
it wuz troo.
jist wanna yoo
scruff tokn.
thirza right
way ti spell
ana right way
ti tok it. this
is me tokn yir
right way a
spellin. this
is ma trooth.
yooz doant no
thi trooth
yirsellz cawz
yi canny talk
right. this is
the six a clock
nyooz. belt up.

(6)

its aw thi
fault a
thi unions hi
said n thi
wurkirs beein
too greedy

hi added n
thi commies n
no inuff
moderates stonnin
upn gettin
coontid n
lame ducks gitn
whut huvyi
bailt oot n
white elifints
getn selt doon
thi river n
a mean
wiv goat tay
puhll in
wur belts n
wur bax ur
tay thi waw
yiv goat tay
admit it.

then hi took
ootiz nummer
eight n
geen a luvvly
wee chip up
right
biside thi flag
n tapptit doon
furra three:

a burdie.

(7)

dispite
thi fact
thit
hi bilonged
tay a
class uv
people
thit hid
hid thir
langwij
sneered
it
since hi
wuz born;

dispite
a long
history uv
poverty n
thi
violence uv
people in
positions
uv
power telln
him his
culture wuz
a sign
of his
inferiority;

thit fur
thi
purposes uv
cultural
statistics hi
didny really
exist; amaz-
in iz it
might seem
this
ordinary wurkn
man got
up wan day
n
wuz herd
tay rimark
thit

it wuzny
sitcha
bad day
tay be
alive

from **Ghostie Men**

(2)

ma lungz iz fuckt
bronchitis again
thi smoakn

lookit
same awl spiht
yella ngreen

van goghs palate
paintn sunflowers

(4)

humpty dumpty satna waw
humpty dumpty hudda big faw

aw thi kingz hoarsyz
inaw thi kingz men

came charjn up
n trampld im inty thi grunn

(5)

mehta physics
fuckin mehta physics
yiwithmi

yi read mi pahl
see that sun therr
see thaht fuckin currnt bun

extreme rashnlist
extreme rashnlist wid doubt
wid doubt fit id rise thimorra

Bertrind Russl
Bertrind Russl ma freend
fuckin right on ih

(7)

would thi prisoner
in thi bar
please stand

fur thi aforesaid crime
uv writn anuthir poem
awarded thi certificate of safety
by thi scottish education department
fit tay be used in schools
huvn no bad language
sex subversion or antireligion
I hereby sentence you
tay six munths hard labour
doon nthi poetry section
uv yir local library
coontn thi fuckin metaphors

(9)

baa baa black sheep
have you any wool
yes sir yes sir
three bags full

one for thi master
n anuthir wan fur thi master
n wan fur thi fuckin church

Design for a commemorative stamp celebrating 1000 years of "The Language Question"

(12)

yonza big wank
fivir a saw wan
mind yi

thi skwerr root
a thi sum
a thi skwerr

a thi two oapasit sides
Ezekiel

sorry

iz eakl
tay thi sum
a thi fuckin
whutivir it iz

upyir crack

(14)

efturryd geenuz iz speel
iboot whut wuz right
nwhut wuz rang
boot this nthat
nthi nix thing

a sayzty thi bloke
nwhut izzit yi caw
yir joab jimmy

am a liason co-ordinator
hi sayz oh good ah sayz
a liason co-ordinator

jist whut this erria needs
whut way aw thi unimploymint
inaw thi bevvyin
nthi boayz runnin amock
nthi hoossyz fawnty bits
nthi wummin n tranquilisers
it last thiv sent uz
a liason co-ordinator

sumdy wia digree
in fuck knows whut
getn peyd fur no known
whut thi fuck ti day way it

(17)

right inuff
ma language is disgraceful

ma maw tellt mi
ma teacher tellt mi
thi doactir tellt mi
thi priest tellt mi

ma boss tellt mi
ma landlady in carrington street tellt mi
thi lassie ah tried tay get aff way in 1969 tellt mi
sum wee smout thit thoat ah hudny read chomsky tellt mi
a calvinistic communist thit thoat ah wuz revisionist tellt mi

po-faced literati grimly kerryin thi burden a thi past tellt mi
po-faced literati grimly kerryin thi burden a thi future tellt mi
ma wife tellt mi jist-tay-get-inty-this-poem tellt mi
ma wainz came hame fray school an tellt mi
jist aboot ivry book ah oapnd tellt mi
even thi introduction tay thi Scottish National Dictionary tellt mi

ach well
all livin language is sacred
fuck thi lohta thim

An Old Story

They invented the concept, and then they invented the concept of their own ownership, of it. They invented the institutions from within which they lent out things to see if others could replicate their fitness-to-own. Fitness to own, they said, resided in the ability to say why and how a thing was or was not a thing-within-the-concept. Only things-within-the-concept had value within the institutions. In owning the concept, they owned the things-within-the-concept, and made their living by them.

They said silly things like, "When we speak of greatness in a literary work we normally do so because we recognise that it has enlarged our knowledge of the nature and capacities of man." By "we" they pretended to mean the whole human race, but really they meant people like themselves who in owning the things-within-the-concept, conceptually owned that which contained the values of the whole human race, in their own terms. From within the institutions they were thus not merely members of the human race, but conceptual owners of its values. This made them feel good.

A maker of a thing was not necessarily a maker of a thing-within-the-concept, and was certainly not an owner of the concept, unless in that separate institutional capacity alone. The maker in his being as a human was only part of that whole human race whose values the owners-of-the-concept conceptually owned. Yet the owners of the concept might choose to make public, or privately to reveal to the maker, any added store of knowledge of the nature and capacities of man, which the maker's made-thing had disclosed. Thus the makers would come to know their place in the Great Chain of Being.

Their place was supposedly within the word owned by the owners of the concept: for the concept was the enclosing word, and ownership of that word had been, and always would be, the irreconcileable opposite

---

a
parasite that
survives by
defining the host
in ways that
maintain its own
habitat

the
institution
of the
state

Honest

A canny even remembir thi furst thing a remembir. Whit a mean iz, a remembir aboot four hunner thingz, awit wance. Trouble iz tay, a remembir thim aw thi time.

A thinka must be gon aff ma nut. Av ey thoat that though – leasta always seemti be thinkin, either am jist aboot ti go aff ma nut, or else am already affit. But yi ey think, ach well, wance yir aff yir nut, yill no no yiraffit. But am no so sure. A wish a wuz.

Even jist sitn doonin writn. A ey useti think, whenever a felt like writn sumhm, that that wiz awright, aw yi hud to say wuz, ach well, a think ahl sit doonin write sumhm, nyi jiss sat doonin wrote it. But no noo, naw. A canny even day that for five minutes, but ahl sitnlookit thi thing, nthink, here, sumdayz wrote that afore. Then ahl go, hawlin aw thi books ootma cupboard, trynti find out hooit wuz. Nwhither a find out or no, it takes me that long luknfurit, a canny be bothird writn any mair, wance av stoapt. An anyway, a tend ti think, if it's wan a they thingz that might uv been writn before, there's no much point in writin it again, even if naibdy actually huz, is there?

It's annoyin – a feel av got this big story buldn up inside me, n ivri day ahl sit down, good, here it comes, only it dizny come at all. Nthi thing iz, it's Noah's if a even no what thi story's goany be about, coz a doant. So a thinkty ma cell, jist invent sumdy, write a story about a fisherman or sumhm. But thi longer a think, thi mair a realise, a canny be bothird writn aboota fisherman. Whut wid a wahnti write about a fisherman fur? N am no gonny go downti thi library nsay, huvyi enny booksn fishermen, jiss so's a can go nread up about thim, then go n write another wan. Hoo wahntsti read a story about fishermen anyway, apart fray people that wid read it, so's they could go n write another wan, or fishermen that read? A suppose right enough, thi trick might be, that yi cin write a story about a fisherman, so long as thi main thing iz, that thi bloke izny a fisherman, but a man that fishes. Or maybe that izny right at all, a widny no. But a do no, that as soon as a lookt up thi map ti see what might be a good name furra fishn village, nthen maybe went a walk ti think up a good name for a fisherman's boat, nthen a sat nworked out what age thi fisherman should be, nhow tall he wuz, nwhat colour his oilskins were, nthen gotim wokn iniz oilskins, doon frae thi village tay iz boat, ad tend ti think, whut duzzy wahnti day that fur? Kinni no day sumhm else wayiz time? Aniffa didny think that ti masell, if a jiss letm go, ach well, it's iz job, away out ti sea, ana big storm in chapter two, ahd tend ti think, either, here, sumdyz wrote that before, or, can a no day sumhm else wi ma time? An in fact, if a came across sumdy sitn readn it eftir a did write it, if a hud, ad tend ti thinkty ma cell, huv they got nuthn behtr ti day wi their time?

A don't no that am sayn whut a mean. But a suppose underneath everythin, thi only person a want ti write about, iz me. It's about time a wrote sumhm aboot masell! But whut? Ah thought even, ach well, jist write doon a lohta yir memories, then maybe they'll take some kinda shape, anyi kin use that ti write a story wi, or a play, or a poem, or a film-script, or God only knows whut, on thi fly. So that's whuta did. Didny mahtr thi order, jist day eftir day, writn doon ma memories. N ad be busy writn it, thinkin, whut an incredible life av hud, even upti noo. Then ad be thinkin, they'll no believe aw this hapnd ti me. Then a looktitit, najistaboot threw up. It wiz nuthin ti day wi me at all. Nthi other people ad be writin about, thi people ad met an that, it wuz nuthin ti day wi them either. It might eveniv been awright, if you coulda said it was about me nthem meetin, but you couldny even say that. It wiz jist a lohta flamin words.

But that's sumhm else. Yi write doon a wurd, nyi sayti yirsell, that's no thi way *a* say it. Nif yi tryti write it doon thi way yi say it, yi end up wi thi page covered in letters stuck thigithir, nwee dots above hof thi letters, in fact, yi end up wi wanna they thingz yid needti huv took a course in phonetics ti be able ti read. But that's no thi way a *think*, as if ad took a course in phonetics. A doant mean that emdy that's done phonetics canny think right – it's no a questiona right or wrong. But ifyi write down "doon" wan minute, nwrite doon "down" thi nixt, people say yir beein inconsistent. But ifyi sayti sumdy. "Whaira yi afti?" nthey say, "Whut?" nyou say, "Where are you off to?" they don't say, "That's no whutyi said thi furst time." They'll probably say sumhm like, "Doon thi road!" anif you say, "What?" they usually say, "Down the road!" the second time – though no always. Course, they never really say, "Doon thi road!" or "Down the road!" at all. Least, they never say it the way it's spelt. Coz it *izny* spelt, when they say it, is it?

A fine point, perhaps. Or maybe it izny, a widny no. Or maybe a think it is, but a also a think that if a say, "Maybe it izny" then you'll turn it over in your head without thinkin, "Who does he think he is – a linguistic philosopher?" Or maybe a widny bothir ma rump whether it's a fine point or it izny: maybe a jist said it fur effect in thi furst place. Coz that's sumhm that's dawned on me, though it's maybe wanna they thingz that yir no supposed ti say. An thirz a helluv a lohta them, when yi think about it, int thir? But anyway, what's dawned on me, or maybe it's jist emergin fray ma subconscious, is, that maybe a write jist tay attract attention ti ma cell. An that's a pretty horrible thought ti emerge fray emdy's subconscious, coz thi nixt thing that emerges is, "Whut um a – a social inadequate?" N as if that izny bad enough, thi nixt thing that yi find yirself thinkin, is, "Am a compensatin for ma social inadequacy, 'by proxy', as it were?" An thi nixt thing, thi fourth thing, that yi find yirself thinkin, is, "If av committed maself, unwittingly, ti compensation 'by proxy', does that mean that a sense a inadequacy, unwittingly, huz become a necessity?" An thi fifth, and thi sixth, an thi seventh thingz that yi find yirself thinkin, are, "Whut if ma compensation 'by proxy' is found socially inadequate?" and "Ivdi's against me – a always knew it," and "Perhaps posterity will have better sense."

Thi apprentice has lifted ma balls an cock," said the plumber. Sorry, that comes later. Am no sayin that these seven thoughts necessarily come in the order in which av presented thim. Ti some people, ahl menshin nay names, these thoughts never emerge fray their subconscious, particularly thi fifth, which is, yi can imagine, thi most terrible thought, of thi lot. Often it turns out that thoughts six and seven are thi most popular, though thoughts one ti five are largely ignored. But thi more yi ignore thoughts one ti five, thi more thoughts six and seven will out. Coz although thought five, "Whut if ma compensation 'by proxy' is found socially inadequate?" never emerges fray yir subconscious, there comes a day when, in a casual discussion about Literature in general, sumdy says, "Your stuff's a lohta rubbish." It might not even be so blunt – in fact, what usually happens is, that in the foyer of a theatre or sumhm, an in thi middle of a casual conversation about Literature in general, then sumdy introduces you ti sumdy else, an thi other person says, "Who?" An although "Who?" might no sound like a literal translation of, "Your stuff's a lohta rubbish," nonetheless, in the thoughts of a social inadequate, it's as near as dammit. So havin secretly thunk thought six, "Ivdi's against me – a always knew it," yi hurry hame ti write sumhm, ti get yir ain back. These ur thi symptoms. Coz yir that fed up wi ivdi yi know, so yi think, that writin sumhm seems about thi only thing worth dayin. Then at least when yir finished yi feel a hell of a lot better, coz whoever it was that was gettin onyir wick before, yi can go upty an say, "A don't gee a damn whut you think about me, coz av jist wrote a poem, an that's sumhm you huvny done. An even if yi huv, albetyi it wuz rotten." Course you don't actually say all that – you don't *huvti* say it, even if yi could be bothered. An if it's sumdy that *did* say ti you, "Your stuffs a lohta rubbish," thirz no much point in goin upti thim anyway, is there? But yi can ey jist look thim in thi eye, in yir mind's eye, an think, "Perhaps posterity will have better sense."

"Ahma writur, your only a wurkur", a said, to thi plumbir.
"Fux sake Joe stick wan on that kunt," said the apprentice.
"Ball an cocks," said the plumber, "Ball an cocks. A firgot ma grammur."
"Gerrihtuppyi," a said, to thi apprentice.
"Lissn pal yoor tea'll be up na minit," said the plumber.
"Couldny fuckin write a bookie's line ya basturdn illiturate," a said, ti the plumber.

"Right. Ootside," said the plumber. "Mawn. Ootside."

Sorry. That comes later.

from Hesitations

(1)

so whut day yi day wi yirsell then ih

whut day yi day these days

* *

really
been a while intit

thats good
that's   ok then ih

ahm thi same

(4)

yi surta
keep trynti avoid it thats
the difficult bitty it

jist
no keep findn yirsell
sitn

wotchn thi telly ur
lookn oot thi windy

that wey yi say
christ a could

go a roll n egg
ur
whuts thi time fuck me

wiv nay
cookn oil nwi need
potatoes

(5)

seen im? seen im?

other times though

fuckin murder eh

couldny turn a

christ ah.

yup

Opting for early retirement

time only/
time management

reified agency
of cost-function conscience

numerical value
constantly

defining the scope
of being-in-the-structure

taboo being
unpredictable being

being as quantum
being as inefficient

motor tasks
establishing targets

recognising actual deficiencies
establishing potential deficiencies

guilty until innocent
the human as an agent of deficiency

the question always
and the answer always

surely total innocence is impossible

firmly

It would be wrong not to say
this is what happened. But

considering all other points of view
as not totally invalid in themselves;

it might be safer to say nothing
about the whole incident, and

rest assured that whatever you or I
may think of it, the matter is closed.

Skills

inventing jobs
teaching the skills

of applying for jobs

—

one of millions
training

to acquire the skills
to apply for jobs

—

not out of a job
but training

to apply for a job
and to be in a job

efficiently

—

co-operating with management
competing with colleagues

learning the ropes

The underfunder's utopia

the state hospital
with one bed

always full
always efficient

doon the close
oot the back door

roon thi
back a thi middens

heh maw
ah shouts heh maw

gonny chuck uz doon
wan a yoan

kitsch kailyard
iconographic

jeelie pieces

ahm clean oota
kitsch kailyard

iconographic
jeelie pieces

shi shouts

flingin doon
the empty jeely jawr

she used tay
get inty the pictures wi

from **Myths in these Parts**

They say in these parts

"When you die,
you go to your granny's."

Your granny sits in the sky
with a bag of white peppermint lumps.

"Come on in," she says,
"You made an awful fuss of it.

We were wondering
when you were coming to see us."

respite in the reading

stepping into that space
out of the past
surrounding
this place, become
an accompanying darkness;

the role, a model
of being oneself, helped
by the places you were
led into, of your own accord.

it never changes, always
changing, this present
become a welcoming
familiar, no time to stay.

the enemy without

bomb them, bomb them!
cries
the editor of the *Catholic Herald*

through a hubbub of cliches
about "appeasement"
"if we had sat back while Hitler"

etc etc etc
the usual

the usual moral outrage

assessments of topography
linked-up tacticians
named & numbered weaponry

– only the demons have changed;

2 a.m.
in a territory without a valid state

where the journalists validate the politicians
and the politicians validate the journalists

listening to the radio
headphoned like an airpilot

while my wife sleeps by my side

MISSILES LAUNCHED FROM MORAL HIGH GROUND

THE PRESENT TENSE

a semi-epistolary romance

Ah, Sun-flower! weary of time

– Blake

Lyk as the dum
Solsequium
With cair ou'rcum

– Alexander Montgomerie

... The ocean, grinding stones,
Can only speak the present tense

– Robert Lowell

This one a fiction. That we knew nothing, ************************** **. The kind that ********** ************************* because we're masochists at heart. That doesn't want to be thought too systematically intelligent, ********* ***************************** To be lovable ***************************** *** then to complain about it, all the time, all the time.

Time – time, time, time, time, time. Better to be drunk and randomly intelligent, ****************************** for which you cannot be held responsible, *************************** and for which you can be held responsible, because you are saying it. So you can be responsible for your intelligence but innocent of it. *********************************** will make you lovable, that in your own innocence ************** **********************************

The model. The model is a model of literature is a model of language is a model of consciousness, that includes reader and writer as existing at the same time. That paradox, that conceit. That's what the fucking model is.

It's the nature of the Present Tense, that's what I've been worrying at this past how long. I made this analysis on DBASE 11 of 100 poems by fifty poets, two each, chosen more or less at random from my shelves. Several lists, poet, poem, tense, reference, attitude, form and so on. Kept thinking of new categories not so much to categorise them as to force myself to articulate my feelings, and to compare poems especially different schools that usually have a brick wall separating them. It took me long enough to notice that fully 95 out of the 100 contained the Present Tense in some form or another. I say in some form or another because of course it wasn't the same Present Tense that was being used at all, yet the type of Present Tense used tended to be the fundament on which the structure was built.

The fundament in that it was that which carried the crunch, one way or another. It was that which let you know where the writer was speaking from, what was the place of address, whether there was room in it for you – and whether the described person, the subject of the poem or whatever, was actually existing in that world or was already stuffed and on the wall for the writer to write the nametag and fill in the habitat.

...I resolved to take a terrible revenge. A hatchet was fetched... whether the shock to the whole framework of the secretary was responsible, I do not know, but I do know that a secret drawer sprang open, one which I had never before noticed. This opened a pigeonhole that I naturally had never discovered. Here to my great surprise I found a mass of papers, the papers which form the content of the present work.

(Kierkegaard: Either/Or)

I think there's something wrong with my liver.

(Dostoevsky: Notes from Underground)

I must apologise for having persuaded my patient to write his autobiography... I take my revenge by publishing them, and I hope he will be duly annoyed.

(Svevo: Confessions of Zeno)

I offer no remarks on it, and make as few additions to it, leaving every one to judge for himself.

(Hogg: Confessions of a Justified Sinner)

These notebooks were found among Antoine Roquentin's papers. We are publishing them without alteration.

(Sartre: Nausea)

And it is only the wish to be useful that has prompted me to publish these fragments of a diary that came into my hands accidentally.

(Lermontov: A Hero of our Time)

Attacked in early youth by an abominable moral malady, I here narrate what happened to me during the space of three years.

(De Musset: The Confessions of a Child of the Century)

I climb onto my bed...Some crumbling cornicing, two loose bricks, some loose plaster; an opening is revealed to my eyes, big as my hand, but invisible from below, due to the cornice-work. I look... I gaze... the room next door presents itself to me, completely exposed.

(Barbusse: Hell)

It takes you to a discussion of literature as a model of diction versus literature as a model of meaning, or lexical intensity; punctuation as a signpost to breath or as organiser of areas of semantic yield. This side of the Atlantic, Finnegan's Wake's the big crossroads followed by Beckett's stuff circa 1945-52. Or maybe not, Mr Wayside Pulpit.

Breath, breath, breath, breath, breath. If only Winnicott had gone further with that aside about the baby's first perception of breath, median between inner and outer, its role as the point at which the defenses are down. Maybe he did, I just haven't seen it. So much of his stuff is great, so exciting to read. All that stuff about the sucking-blankets (his "guggie", mine used to call it) "transitional objects" and their relation to culture, the first experience of symbols in time. That "potential space" where play occurs... "It is play that is the universal, and that belongs to health." Good on you, Mr Winnicott. A very healthy man.

---

30 WED Ironic those most concerned to emphasise the importance of what is called "orature" are often the people most hostile to any indication of oral pronunciation. There is literature, and there is the oral. The oral written down is orature. But there must be no vestige of the orality emphasised in the transcription. This would be as it were to move to the viscous, the existential, away from Word as thing in itself which is pronounced. Word is a serious thing, its serious thingness should not be threatened by the interpolation of that which would leave the vestige of utterance as part of its description. To indicate the act of the individual speaker in the utterance is to "debase" the word and to question the common reality of that to which it refers.

There is a congruence here with conservative folklorists who like to see themselves as defenders of the true People's Culture against all these experimentalists, elitist wankers etc. "Orature" is taken as having an inbuilt duty to be revered, though you always know you're in the presence of Death when reverence and art are bound together. It's reverence for the Word supposedly common to orature and literature that arouses hostility and a defensive contempt when a viscous link between the two is presented. One reason is that indication of pronunciation drags the present into that past from which the Word is supposed unobtrusively to have been launched. It is vital to protect the pastness of that past, because in so doing one can present the fixity and inevitability of tradition. The function of the artist is to act "responsibly" towards that fixed tradition, and a fixed tradition is insecure without the fixity of Word. Hence to challenge that fixity of word by site-specifying it in the mouth of a particular speaker, is to behave "irresponsibly".

Trouble with people who identify the unconscious with a linguistic structure I think is that it can so easily drift into this authority-based thing. It's that perennial tendency you always have to be on your guard against, those who want to construct a "natural law" that's prescriptive. Or as somebody I read once put it, whenever moralists have recourse to biology you know there's a reactionary viewpoint coming up.

Have you read Eriugena, the Irish 9th century geezer? Not that I've learnt him off by heart myself, but he's got some prrretty interesting things to say about words, thought, all that sort of trade. He thinks our very own Blessed Trinity, which is to say Evans Stein and Peacock (sorry, that's facetious) has a structure that corresponds to the structure of language and its relation to thought. Reminds me of some of our twentieth century bods in his own way. Not that I'd ever say anything about him in public of course you know the way it is unless you can name every stop between Auchenshuggle and Clydebank you're not supposed to get on the tram. "Ignorance of the divine nature is true wisdom; by not knowing it is best known." That's Eriugena, or John Scotus to you. Of course you'll put it down to "the rhetorical nihilism of the Celt".

MacNeice	Woods	Pa+Pr	"these Woods are", we walk out we?
MacSweeney	Ode Grey Ros	Pres	"damn is dam" "revives" among rand imag
MacSweeney	Ode Stem Hai	Pres	"phantoms energise" etc imag/paint const
Magill	La Basee Rd	Pres	what "I" sold hear each night+ addr read
Muldoon	The Sightsee	Past	n/a
Muldoon	Cherish the	Pr+Pa	double"as it is" "in this poem he opens"

Neruda	Walking Arou	PrFsu	"I want to see no more" images of destr
Neruda	The Portrait	Pa+Pr	Mem of persecuted + in stone "he lives"
Olson	Maximus, to	Pa+Pr	rem + rep "we grow up many" here "I look"
Olson	The Kingfish	Pr+Pa	multiple, hist + opinion + un & sp desc
Paulin	Descendancy	Pres	Un.opinion + cousin drives + "could be"
Paulin	Foot Patrol,	Apres	mid after "they hold" rifles+morWhyisit
Raworth	Conscience o	Pres	image-reflections "in this ward" etc
Raworth	Wandering	Upr.H	"lost and am fishing" selfaddr images
Redgrove	Rescue	Pres	unclear imag-seq The doctor booms
Redgrove	Florent	Past	n/a
Rosenberg	Returning We	Pr+Pa	"night is", we hear, + univ ab girls
Rosenberg	Through Thes	Pres	Jews "these cold days" "They see"
Rothenberg	Pirate, The	Pa+Pr	narr of pilgrim "who eats iron?" etc
Rothenberg	Poland 1931-	Upres	dram mon address to poland "my mind is"
Sorescu	The Glass Wa	Pa+Pr	berlin wall allegory, in which we live
Sorescu	The Complain	Past	dram mon "here at the last judgement"
Stevens	The Public S	Pr+Pa	described archit "as when a jan bears"
Stevens	Of Modern Po	Upres	Of poetry, what "It has to be living"etc
Thomas D	And Death Sh	Fut	n/a

---

how cum
the how dumb deid
ach
let me take yi back
tay the midnineteen sixties
the setting is glasgow
gateway to barrhead
the birthplace of john davidson
headbanger and poet
who is irrelevant to our tale
the setting is glasgow
the place a bookshop

ach
robbe-grillet
notes from underground
the divided self
gide's journals
pascal's pensees
edward glover
either/or
watt and molloy
a hero of our time
ach
these books and others

birling in the head
of the hero of our tale
lonely in a bookshop
sexually fucked up
given to hard drinking
and little ambition
not yet political
not yet in london
not yet with a baby
and a landlord
who didn't like babies
or rent books   ach

About government, in relation to what you say. I have a book out the university library just now, a very exciting read, a book from which I will be taking some notes before returning it. The book is called "Lobbying Government" and is by far the clearest guide to the actual wielders of power in government that I have come across. It is written, with the help of M.P.s and government officials, by an advisor aiming the book at corporate directors wishing to use the government, as he puts it, "as a tool." It is not a left-wing book, which makes for very interesting reading of such as the table (the book is full of clear tables) which lists on a mark-out-of-ten basis those who have actual power: the single M.P. is bottom of the league (1 out of 10) whilst the Commons Chamber amasses 2 out of 10: comment "Facade of democracy". The new policy of farming out government officials to private industry before they then go back into government, of course also makes for interesting reading, as is the layer of industrialist "policy advisors." Not that the book names names but if you read the business pages of the papers at all there's plenty to choose from. The deliberate blurring of the distinction between industrialist and government official is shown in Scotland just now – the so-called "plan for growth" operated by a group of major industrialists as official advisors whose companies happen to have given the Tory Party hundreds of thousands of pounds. There's our Minister of Health who just happens to have made £30,000 in director's fees from advising on private tenders into the health service, the year before he took office. There's the latest "leak" from the Department of Overseas Aid, which makes it known that the government wishes, along with the Americans, to launch a scheme by which those countries requiring aid could have "help" to have their nationalised industries privatised. There's the latest news, within the past few days, of the "consortium" that is bidding to take over the General Electric Company, a huge thing worth billions, in the care of which there are a lot of Britain and America's most advanced and secret military work. The head of G.E.C. is, or was till recently a former government minister. The chairman of the consortium making the bid is the former Minister of Defence.

One could go on, and on.

---

10 SUNDAY Literature as dialogue. To travel anywhere, past and present, in equality of dialogue. Area of encounter as hologram. As model of the universe. As agora. This time no exclusions. First slave to

be freed, the reader. Three dimensional plan, to which added the dimension of personal existence, which is inseparable from Time.

The usual straight-line metaphors of tradition's path, course etc. Their relation to imposed concepts of deviance. Their invalidation of personal existence.

Blake's "Mock On Mock On". The kinetics of the thought of the first two verses. The argument between images of directioning and two-dimensionality. The three-dimensionality of "Israel's tents" in the last verse. The world in the grain of sand.

As^{1} k^{2}ingf^{3}isher^{4}s^{1} c^{2}atch f^{3}ir^{4}e, d^{5}r^{4}agonf^{3}lies d^{5}r^{4}aw f^{3}lame
As tumbled over rim on roundy wells
Stones ring; like each tucked string tells, each hung bell's
Bow swung finds tongue to fling out broad its name;
Each mortal thing does one thing and the same
Deals out that being indoors each one dwells;
Selves – goes itself; myself it speaks and spells,
Crying, What I do is me: for that I came.

Ring out wild bells: – ing, ing, ing, ung, ung, ung, ing, ing, ing, ing/
ells, ells, ells, eals, ells, elves, elf, elf, ells –

Copleston: "It is not so easy to understand exactly what this *haecceitas* or *entitas singularis vel individualis* or *ultima realitas entis* actually is. It is, as we have seen, neither matter nor form nor the composite thing. A human being, for instance, is *this* composite being, composed of *this* matter and *this* form... it seems to be implied that a thing has *haecceitas* or 'thisness' by the fact that it exists."

CLASS middle **y/n** working **y/n** ex-working educated tertiary **y/n** **REFERENCE** topical/real world/ interpretation of events/ politics/ in the world/ restricted world **PREOCCUPATIONS** domestic / ideological/ academic **VOICE** shouted / quiet / interior / exterior / earnest / private school / comprehensive / commitment **y/n** anger **y/n** personal **y/n** group implied **y/n** honest **y/n** **BREATH** private / public-declam / personal / narrative / dramatic / exact of diction **y/n** sentences **y/n** utterance **y/n** intimate / self revelatory / fake self revelatory **EMOTION** primary **y/n** humour **y/n** personal irony **y/n** despair **y/n** sarcastic **y/n** presumed shared anger **y/n** **TONE** earthy / gutsy / exasperated / tender / beautiful / self deflating / self aggr-andising / self disappearing / self hiding / trying to convince you / assuming you're not there/ tone the justification for hidden premises **PERSON** evidently present / secondary / male – build / female – building / persona-isolating / isolates others / subjects presumed to be not part of audience / part of group / group in audience presumed / men **y/n** women **y/n** race **y/n** class **y/n** disdain for w/c culture **y/n** disdain for m/c culture **y/n** presumed victim / hetero **y/n** gay **y/n** whiffy **y/n** **SEX** lust / abstracted / pantheist / life-force / metaphysical / coded for audience approval / difficult to think of this writer having sex / tone that suggests passion is inferior **MEANING** overt / disguised / presumed / fake "objective" / difficult to understand / specific concrete / abstract nouns as subject / thing primary / detailed / provides information / moral primary / moralist / parable maker / subject as instance of a moral / **VERIFYING AUTHORITY** structure **y/n** social group **y/n** person **y/n** culture **y/n** coded for integration-into-larger-model etc **y/n** anti-integratory **y/n** **PLACE** poetry hall / pub / church / classroom / street / where the reader is / **TOPOGRAPHY** domestic / industrial / rural / national / urban / allegory / literary / real environment / environment as parable / **VARIETY** tone **y/n** reference **y/n** structure **y/n** rhythm **y/n**

Anyway. As the chap says, From Coppernickers to Warhole, "we have witnessed the destabilisation of the subject of the subject-centred universe and the rise of a cultural physics that places the mobility of the sign at the de-centred centre of all discourses." Which is to say, Fuck me with a broombrushed Mars Bar. "Wot is a wery phallocentric remark, Samivel." Shall we go? (They run like fuck.)

PERSON CENTRED VERSUS AUTHORITY CENTRED

> Present tense meaning recurring things, given constants abstract and concrete
>
> Present tense meaning the present day, contemporary events etc
>
> Present you're in yourself, specific consciousness here & now
>
> Present the thing's in, i.e. as object
>
> Present inside the thing, language of personae etc
>
> Present the narrator's in
>
> Present the author's in, specific there & then
>
> Planck's constant

Whether each has access to the other. e.g. is a persona caged in a present tense inside the present tense of the narrator, reified in a defining action beyond whose perimeter there is no exit. The stereotype as false universal. Existence given in supposed universal present between writer and reader – on condition that a spurious "archetype" is denied access to similar possibilities of time.

Sterne: "I leave this void space that the reader may swear into it any oath that he is accustomed to."

"Mach's book" illusion. Retinal movement not a necessary factor. cf prosody link between line ending and pause, vide Olson's ubiquitous projective verse essay. V-day also 1909 Encyc. Brit. entry on projective geometry. Bon voyage!

```
   /|\     /|\     /|\
  / | \   / | \   / | \
 /  |  \ /  |  \ /  |  \
|  / \  |  / \  |  / \  |
| /   \ | /   \ | /   \ |
|/     \|/     \|/     \|
```

If I would have begun this sentence with a conditional pluperfect subjunctive, it is the ambiguity of "this" that allows me to conclude in the present.

...And so on.

I had this idea about juxtaposing particle, wave, string; noun, verb, sentence; phoneme, morpheme, word. "Wire it all up to synaptic function. Plug all the bastards in to the double helix. The male as particle, the female as wave. Puir wee particles. Always trying to be a straight line."

"But what is now? There is no such thing in physics; it is not even clear that 'now' can ever be described, let alone explained, in terms of physics." The contradiction in a sentence like, "I am presently thinking." That shortfall to infinity, ten to the power minus twenty four seconds, and still travelling. Not that it's the subatomic concept of virtual time or something that bothers me. It's the here-and-now size almost just big enough to understand, that I never understand.

Parliament. The ritualisation of the concept of dialogue. Imprimatur. Nihil obstat. Toot toot, sweetie pie.

---

ablative absolute

having been seized with the dry boke
at the state opening of parliament

black rod delicately applied
the instrument of his nomenclature

to the back of his throat

situations theoretical and contemporary

(1)

somewhere between stocks & shares
and the "commensensical" editorial

pity the poor arts page
thinking itself alone

(2)

The schooner The Mother of Parliaments has anchored in the bay.
The first British ship has reached your land.

See the row-boat, pulling to the shore.
See the ballot-boxes, glinting in the sun!

Run and tell your fellow-tribesmen.
We are going to have a referendum!
Shall we join the British Empire?

(3)

Today is National Income Card-Carrying Day.
On this day all citizens must wear cards prominently declaring their
  total income from all sources for the previous twelve months.

How full the underground shelters are this morning.
All those advocates of “tighter control of the money supply”.
And there is that expert on “international terrorism”.
Quite a card, eh?

Quick though - there goes the Chancellor of the Exchequer.
Oh dear. No pep-talk today!

(4)

You are tracing the link between existential angst and male sexual guilt.
From the consciousness of guilt to the guilt of consciousness.
From Dostoevsky to Sartre.

Your audience this morning is from the “Third World”.
Their bodies are skeletal.
Their eyes seem very large.

One approaches the rostrum.
Food. Food.

(5)

Dear Member: The Party for the Political Advancement of the Upwardly Mobile Sons and Daughters of Parents who were Working Class again requests five dead metaphors and five banal alliterations for inclusion in our party leader’s keynote speech to forthcoming annual party conference. Four acceptances again guarantee admission to conference, with the opportunity to participate in the ten-minute standing ovation at the end of the speech itself.

Last year's poll-toppers, “The demise of the dreary dogmatist” and “A return to radical realism,” remain eligible.

Bon appetit!

(6)

You have returned to Glasgow after a long exile.
A Glasgow Herald special edition is selling like hot cakes.
It publishes a Turkish poet's abstruse new song.

This Turkish poet is of an international cast of mind.
He also has an unselfconscious enjoyment of working-class culture.
In fact his song is about a match between Glasgow Celtic and Glasgow Rangers.

A certain Professor MacFadyen has detected the influence of MacDiarmid.

(7)

as I was waiting upon a bus in Byres Road
musing upon the echtness of the glasgow cultural renaissance

an elderly gentleman came walking by with a smile
who bid good morning to a woman of slightly more tender years
who smiled in reply and said

and how is the wee dog this morning mister mackay

THE PRESS

as

bogus phatic communion

let's not pretend it's dialogue!

(8)

It is five years since the edict "Only the trauchle is clean".
Now the Inspector of Literature himself has sent his Collected Trauchles for review.

Grimly but morally refreshed you reach page five-hundred-and-eighty-three.

"There is not a spark of humour throughout this wholly admirable book," you begin your review. "Nor has irony caused its customary obfuscation through bad faith."

(9)

The administrative resource base of school focused projects and the college-initiated curriculum in the field provides in-service whole-school comprehensive packages for the formulation, implementation and evaluation of major new initiatives developed within the time constraints appropriate to areas of deprivation.

The new multi-purpose role of language across the curriculum will promote the acquisition of subject-specific concepts designed to support and underpin the implementation participation and development of supportive group structures relevant to the mutual interchange of the specific school situation in the context of the community. The conceptual structure of investigative skills will be developed in relation to the creation of dynamic self-initiated visits to explore, redefine and extend criterion-referenced modules for individual problem-solving processes. This should facilitate the co-ordination and liaison of relevant core teams in providing an impetus to integrate in-service evaluation as part of the monitoring and review of inter-dependent consultancy approaches on a one-to-one basis.

(10)

The coach-driver makes an announcement.
"Your poems should have one of two titles:
'The Vanity of Human Wishes', or 'There But for the Grace of God'."

The passengers are excited.
Who will win the word processor? Will it be me?
The lights turn to green. The bus moves off at last.

Let the tour of the slums begin!

(11)

We have decided to make Scotland secure.
This is strategically essential.
No question.

Scottish people have nothing to fear.
Noise pollution should not be a problem.
And all construction work will be landscaped.

We have decided to make America secure.
This is strategically essential.
No question.

Scottish people have nothing to fear.
Noise pollution should not be a problem.
And all construction work will be landscaped.

(12)

Scotland has become an independent socialist republic.
At last.

Eh?
You pinch yourself.
Jesus Christ. You've slept in again.

(13)

And their judges spoke with one dialect,
but the condemned spoke with many voices.

And the prisons were full of many voices,
but never the dialect of the judges.

And the judges said:
"No-one is above the Law."

THE is the father

this is the holy spirit

a is the son

leaning forward

partly the
inside maybe

the outside
of it, who knows

which
is the which

of it, the real
base line

the hologram
liveable within:

it changes
so readily,

the sense
of

the place
you come

to a constant,
gone, no

coming back
again, maybe

all in the head...

Before the 1820 rising in the West of Scotland a network of

don't call them government spies

call them MI5
call them MI6
call them special branch
call them the anti-terrorist squad
call them F1, F2, F3, F4, F5, F6 right through to 12
call them counter-insurgency

don't mention them
keep quiet about them
refuse to discuss how much money's spent
refuse to discuss what they do
swear everyone to secrecy

call them Intelligence

call the critics "unpatriotic"
call the critics "a security risk"
call the critics "conspiracy theorists"
call the critics "traitors"

call the critics *paranoid*

government spies kept watch over the Combination Acts against assembley

four football haiku

Bovril Zen

hawf time
n wan hawn clappin
whair the fuck um ah

auld an firm

a blue sky
a green grunn
an a bowl a hatred

playground football

a hawnfu a boays
n two jaickits
three an in

this sporting life

doon three wan
a rid raw wind
nthi ref a bastard

a could eata   hoarss
a hoarss   a hoarss
my kingdom furra hoarss

from "Foodies" – 1

rest assured

the cattle in our pies
were once
professors of psychiatry

from "Foodies" – 2

GLORIOUS WEATHER IN A TEACUP
TEMPERATURE 90 DEGREES

from "Foodies" – 3

ahma hoarss

"Je Suis un Cheval" - Hans Arp

ahm oan a train
packt ti thi gunnilz
ma compartmints fuhll
a wummin n ivri seat
a man oan ivri wummins knee
helluva hoat
lik sumhm oot thi tropics
aw thi passengers
fuhlln thir faces
champin away
when thi men aw suddnly girn
they wahnt thir mammy's tit
wahnt thir feed
wahnt thir sook
they oapn thi wummins blouses
lift oot the diddies
sook away fur life
fuhll thimsellz wi good fresh mulk
ahm thi only wan no breastfeedin
n naibdy's sookn it me
n am no sitn oan emdy's knee
an naibdyz sittn oan mine
coz ahma hoarss
sitn straight up a big hoarss
ma hinn legs
upnthi seat
leanin nice n comfy
oan ma front legs
nay bothir a nieeeeeei gh gh gh
oan ma breast six buttns
shiny sixy sex appeal
neat n a row
lik glossy buttns n a uniform
how toaty thi world
how mega its cherries

the mainstream...

: a clerisy :

nora's place

a poem in 17 aspects

(1)

across the park, walking
I can't be bothered
making the dinner, going through
all the routines and subroutines

setting it up with the radio at
four to do the peeling, work out
what the rota's been of

food this past week or so
is it time again for fish

trying to get the girls
not eat before dinner
when they come in from school

(2)

I protest at this place
with no people in it

objects for reproducing images
people not actually present

from this wall to this wall
and this wall to this wall

(3)

yes I'm all for him
becoming union rep
– don't let them get away with it!

obviously the last settlement
was a complete sell-out
                                        but then,
aren't most union leaders like that?

on the executive, hobnobbing
far too much with managers
                              first-name terms
                              and they're always
paid far more than the worst off
who need the union most

Dives and Lazarus
that's what we agreed
last night at dinner time

(4)

soon it will be
the familiar footsteps
time sometimes from the

bottom of the stairs the
voices drift up maybe

if you happen to look out the window
at the right time, it is the right time

for a wave. the wave.
people are coming home.
                                        home to

the place that has not existed
these past hours

(5)

if they're finding

the dinner school portions too wee it
must be the cutbacks that'll mean
they'd better come home at

the back of half twelve every
day I'll better maybe
keep a big pot of soup on the

go or get in some
frozen packets hamburgers
fish fingers that sort of thing

you can't give them
chips twice a day though it
wouldn't be a healthy

diet maybe I'll try to
get them go back to dinner school
take pieces with them though

to eke it out

(6)

I don't know what we share exclusively now
other than the children

the best time was when we shared the same political outlook
exclusively   but now

you've others you can do that with
the shared anger at injustice
can be had elsewhere

(7)

the main thing to have controlled
contempt for the idea of
breakdown which is completely

unromantic and painful despite
its aura and pseudo visionary crap about
insights usually obsessive petty

vanities to do with god and the
devil and one-dimensional trains
of thought that go on and on and

people don't understand you any better
at the end of it

(8)

through the
revolving turnstile
past

tomatoes
mushrooms peppers
potatoes

cheese island
milk margarine
yoghurt

pizzas jams marmalades
beans peas carrots
pulses sauces

coffee tea
spaghetti
hoops spam tuna

salmon
ambrosia creamed rice
soups

cornflakes
all bran shredded
wheat fruit

juice soda stream
cooking oil
disposable bin liners

brillo dettol
washing soda crystals
elastoplast toothpaste

kleenex toilet rolls
soap powders fairy
liquid

dog food
birds eye codsteaks
hamburgers

frozen turkey
chicken
new zealand lamb

biscuit alley
fresh fish
on the spot baking

stand
leaning on the trolley
waiting

(9)

nora drinks too much

sometimes one beer is enough to make her go
what is it about nora's drinking

nora creates an environment in which she is approved
if she sits with drinkers, her being a drinker is approved
she is "finally approved simply for what she is"

nora is allowed out the house twice a week
nora's terms are that she doesn't sit with males
nora doesn't want to sit with males anyway
nora sits with alice and betty, who are always there

when nora gets to the Whistler's Dog, alice and betty
approve of her coming

(10)

now he has an affair of the soul elsewhere
now he has the chance to be "as free as himself"
that is what it's about, the sense to be "as free as himself"

maybe to be as free as himself, he has to have the mother at home

* * *

when will nora become herself
when will nora feel "as free as herself"

is nora "just another person"?

(11)

you get that way you get
scared to go out –
                                        don't you:

just that way that
you find yourself putting off
going to the butchers or
                                                        the newsagents;

that thing about
                                    just talking,
where do you put your eyes:
where do you put your eyes
when you're
                                    just talking?

people can tell when you're
                                    not good at it, look

surprised and a bit hurt

(12)

lying looking sideways up
at the bedside photo of my youngest

strange to see that smile
that same set of features
on the face of a woman of fifty

looking back into the room
on an occasion I will never know

long after I'm dead

(13)

out there
in sexual space

deep in the darkness
breath and rhythm

moving to join
into our orb

(14)

how quirky I am
but

I'm not a table
or a pen
or a hill

I'm just a human being
totally representative
as anyone is
outside the self

(and in it)

I wish you would touch me more
it makes me feel happy
and secure

(15)

here she comes,
                    down the stairs
slowly, shopping bag in hand

trying not to think
of the heart-beat, the shallow speed
of the breathing

do you listen to your breath

who on earth
tries to control their breath
on their way to the shops

nora's place
nora's place
nora's place
nora's place
nora's place
nora's place
nora's place
nora's place
nora's place
nora's place
nora's place
nora's place
nora's place
nora's place

nora's place
nora's place
nora's place

nora's place nora's place
nora's place nora's place
nora's place nora's place

nora's place nora's
place nora's place
nora's place nora's
place nora's place
nora's place nora's
place nora's place
nora's place nora's
place nora's place
nora's place nora's
place nora's place
nora's place nora's
place nora's place

nora's place nora's place
nora's place nora's place
nora's place nora's place

(17)

only this particular
street to walk the length

of, this
is not a metaphor, only

being suddenly
walking down a street

in this place, having
this particular sense
not of anxiety, but

“the fact of the presence of existence”

* *

each time it happens
it seems

that all the intervening times
have disappeared

and this
is all that nora really is

A Night at the Pictures

Some time ago my wife Sonya and myself went to the Glasgow Film Theatre, formerly the Cosmo. We went to see a French film called *Jean de Florette*, which had received some good reviews. Unfortunately between our house and the cinema, my wife and myself had a row. I cannot remember what it was about, or any of the details, but as we entered the cinema she delivered a particularly wounding remark, in a quiet voice. I was not going to sit having a night-out as if nothing had happened, but to storm out would have been histrionic. As the film began I therefore found that I was staring at a position on the ceiling somewhere north-west, five to eleven, of the screen itself.

The position of my head was such that a person who did not have a sight of my eyes would have assumed that I was watching the film. I did not want to disturb anyone else in the cinema by making a public issue of my estrangement from the communal event. Gradually I began to "take in" where I was—without moving my position other than the occasional quasi-relaxational shift that would divert potential awareness in others of an unnatural rigidity in one of the group.

The dialogue that filled the theatre seemed a little harsh and loud, as if it needed some adjustment to the volume and the treble.

Also the words were in French, which did not help me, as I only understand it at a simple level, spoken slowly. There were long periods without dialogue, the sound of what was perhaps a cow, of people breathing. Feet on floors, utensils, sounds that indicated a scene indoors. Voices evidently shouting from a distance meant that the action had moved once more outside. The most dramatic point was when the cinema was suddenly filled with the sound of a thunderstorm, while a man shouted at the top of his voice, then started weeping. All the while I kept my eyes averted from the screen. A couple of times my wife asked me if I was alright. I replied that I was.

Away from the screen, the quality of light that the screen threw on the walls and ceiling was surprisingly mixed, jumpy, changing all the time; I could see varied light on the crowns of people near the front, the varying darkness at the small of their backs. Inevitably—I was in an end seat in the balcony—I could see angled shoes at the aisle's edge opposite, the usual light at the carpet shining on a man's ankle. But it was the silence that really struck me: the silence of a building that was not the talking wall at which I couldn't look. The door with its sign EXIT—saying nothing. The building revealed itself as a wall of silence, literally, between the screen and the world. This in the red light that shone faintly on my wife and myself, noticeable in the darker moments, from one of the pinlights above us.

Then it was over, and we were out. I felt I had maybe gone beyond a mark, broken a primitive taboo between friends. But to have called it the breaking of a taboo would maybe have been to load it with a significance it did not deserve. After all, it had just been a huff. When asked how I had enjoyed the film, I had to admit that I had not seen any of it. But by the time we had reached home, I had been told most of the story, and the row was already almost forgotten.

Months later the sequel to *Jean de Florette*—a film called *Manon des Sources*—came to the same cinema. We decided about eight o'clock one evening to go, and got to the cinema just after the film began at half past. We were sitting in the forward region, in the last row of what is called the front section of the theatre. We were in a good mood. No question of a row tonight.

After a while my wife remarked that the opening seemed to be the same as the last one. I thought that perhaps this was a run-through, a kind of reminder of what had taken place in Part One. Or else it was employing the device of beginning and ending the film with the same images, to make some artistic point—like Polanski's *Repulsion*, or the sound of the car crash in Losey's *Accident.* But this was not the case.

It was simply that for the benefit of those who had not seen the film before, the cinema was showing *Jean de Florette* today, Wednesday. The sequel *Manon des Sources* would be shown on Thursday, Friday and Saturday. We had made a mistake.

But my wife had enjoyed the film on its first showing, and she generously agreed that we should just sit there again. So the sounds that had formed for me an incomprehensible abstract were now united with their visual images. I was a member of the audience with my companion, and saw nothing of what I had seen so stealthily before.

Triptych

for those of us
who have to live
outside the
narrative

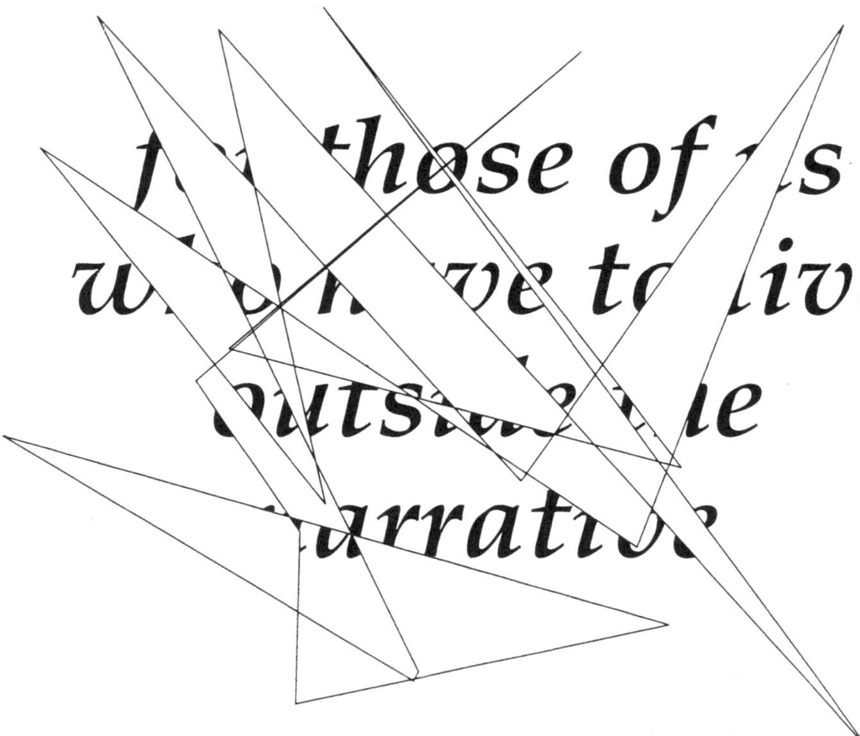
for those of us
who have to live
outside the
narrative

to have access to the silence

to feel part of the silence that is part of that which shares you and not-you

to feel not liable to be attacked at an ontological level

to sense being as not being deprived of being

to sense that it is ok, whatever the it is that is a way of describing you

to sense the it as being something that includes all of your being from the time you were born

to sense the it as being something that includes all of your being from the time you were born

to sense that it is ok, whatever the it is that is a way of describing you

to sense being as not being deprived of being

to feel not liable to be attacked at an ontological level

to feel part of the silence that is part of that which shares you and not-you

to have access to the silence

in hospital

I like seeing nurse frieda knitting
as I like watching my wife knitting
as I liked watching my mother knitting
though she was more of a dabber
(plain and purl, plain and purl)

it's not
"women being in their place"
or knitting the chains that keep them down

just

the future, knitting the future

the present peaceful, quiet
as if

the same woman knitting
for a thousand years

suite On the Page

the local is the international
the national is the parochial

(1)

It looks like
instead of "Scottish Literature"
it has to be "anti-colonial studies"
or some such: fair enough–

if the narrative doesn't fit,
fuck it then. let's instead
have some kind of
discussion, let alone

a "colloquium",
on the function of relative
spacing and relative articulat-
ion in, the place of address:

which is to say:-
the page itself.

(2)

down this way
following
the line

of breathing,
starting over

again and
again and again

it does not turn
without

that which
carries it
over (and over)

(3)

it's too easy

saying
"the craft"

defines
thing-in-itself

unique
to current instance:

but how otherwise
assess

the given syntactic
the visual plane

the page
where pacing can be articulated

(4)

it seems that it's always
the same setting out, the same
standing still in the one voice
looking at it:

                    hello again.
ears not chooned to listen
outside of the word,
                  to skate between
and away from the trampo-

line

and does it matter? maybe not:
let's head off together in this
little soliloquy:

play some music if you're lucky–
if that's who you are, today

(5)

the way of it
is not always forward:

it can sometimes
be less than that which you admire;

but being there, with it
or is it on it, who knows

eventually
the thing itself, is:

this the way
it occurs

(6)

why it should be this way
                    god only knows
if there was one–or many

whoever invented this position
this way of being
                              –living on the page

in a voice that nobody knows, nor
wants to know: who invented it, who
invented all this

this at least we do together
                      not
"the royal we"   you know...
                      but

(7)

this is the way
I think we want it
to operate: not

crowding the page
as some larger font:

but using simply
that which seems
easiest on the eye,

having in mind
the relative possibilities

of particular spacing, hallmark
of that lowercase tradition
we long admire

(8)

turning salty the
way
the unknown

which way turns
listening

partly
the waters
undivided

between
the self
beckoning

back again

(9)

various
the abstract

climbs down
reckoning

always never
the same, whenever

it lands itself
meaning taken

over, moving
over and out

(10)

turning around
and around
finding

the only
place left

the day
the page

another one

(11)

the day
closes

it comes
to its way

of
this being

the end

the case for lower case

lower case posits *in-the-presence-of*
lower case is presence
lower case is company

lower case can jump from one proposition to another
across the page

lower case does not spurn its friends in the typesetting office
lower case may yet lean on a semi-colon for breath; on its way up the stairs

lower case listens to the voice of the people
lower case is not Edict
lower case is the kinesis of democracy

CAPITAL is stasis
CAPITAL is closure of the business in hand
CAPITAL is the cumulation of reified density
CAPITAL has no being at its centre
CAPITAL is without breath

the CAPITALIST SENTENCE begins by setting out its Stall
the CAPITALIST SENTENCE has the subject as line-manager of the verb
the CAPITALIST SENTENCE has no room in which to move
at the end of a CAPITALIST SENTENCE the world comes to a full stop.

THE CAPITALIST SENTENCE IS A DEATH SENTENCE.

lower case gives you space to live
lower case makes peace with the living
lower case does not hide behind the toga of the Roman Empire
lower case is the swish of the skirt

hmm
always here
as natural as breathing

lower space.....lower space..... lower space......lower space

FIN

the pact

I have to discover
who

I'm talking to,
the residue

of this present less
the present questioning :

what borrowed
from the memory

addresses itself;
the memory

undisturbed for years
a subject-object

relationship:
a sentence at last

a sentence with a silence in it
- and at the end of it

June the Second

it is dawn and my wife is coming to bed
and she has been watching a film about the life of charlie parker

and the air in the bedroom is silent while she undresses
and the light is there at the side of the curtain beyond her head

and she tells me his body gave up of drink and drugs when he was 34
and I decide I am awake and go to the kitchen for a drink of water

and the sky in the north is translucent like a lake
translucent like a lake though it is only 3 am

and when I go back we lightly hold hands as we sometimes do
until the first to be falling asleep begins to twitch and tonight it's Sonya

and I withdraw my hand and lie back looking at the ceiling
I am aged 51 years and nine months and nine to ten days

touching your face

with that
silence

it creates
allowing

and
trusting

the allowed;
all that's

been said
and is saying

this time
breath

held
between us

each time
familiar

each time
new

Kierkegaard

true to the place
of doubt

necessary: integrity
of purpose before all—

the crowd is the untruth
he said

and forsooth he spake wisely
in that trice

Remembrance Day

I know what it is
to be powerless

I know what it is
to be made to lie low

while the unknown enemy
invades you

what it is
not to have words

for what is happening
for grass and tree

and inanimate thing
to be

your only witness
on the clearest day

of a childhood
almost fifty years ago;

how I hate
male

fucking violence.
this day

I will wear
nor white nor red

nor count myself solitary
instead

I remember the many
who know what it is

to be made to lie low
while the enemy

known or unknown
invades

in dead of night
or in the field

that spoil of war
that
earth's oldest currency

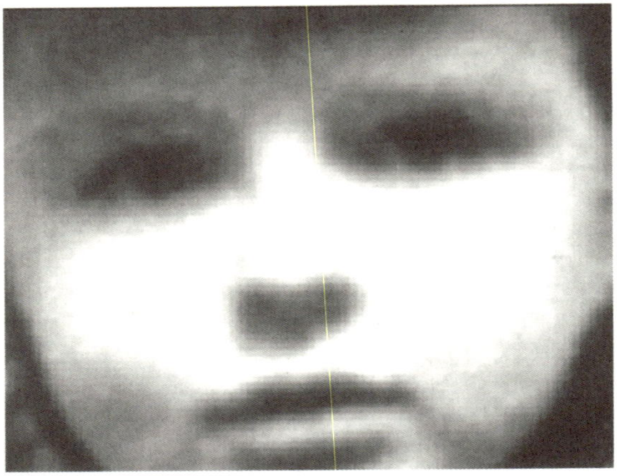

who want
my smile

themselves
their inner child

so to beguile
why

do adults lie

The Fair Cop

a cop came to see me
but I didn't know he was a cop
I'm so trusting!!
and I said sit down and have a cup of tea
and he sat down and had a cup of tea

and he was a young man
a nice looking young man
he reminded me of my son
the taller of my sons
very discreet
a good listener

and I said would you like a banana?
I eat bananas like a gorilla
but the cop didn't want a banana
he asked me if it was all right to use a dictaphone
and I said of course though I don't really like dictaphones

and he was interested in all my life
and he wanted to get a few things straight
it would help him with his work
and I'm getting old
there's bits of me beginning to pack up and go
and I like helping the young
it is one of the pleasures of old age
what else is there for the old to do?

so I told him all I could
and I was very free and honest

I like being free and honest
I like those days when it all comes together
and you know your own story
and you know your own place in the world
and what you have done and why

and he didn't say very much
come to think of it he didn't say very much at all
but he had a nice smile
and he seemed a good listener
so I talked and I talked instructing the young on my path through life

and only once did his expression change somehow
only once did his eyes sort of flicker
and that was when I was talking about terrorism
and how they all use the word terror now instead
and I told him I noticed when the change first took place

I said I remember it being Ariel Sharon
how he kept saying terror terror terror terror
fighting terror war on terror fighting terror war on terror
all instead of terrorism

and now the word's over here

and how this reminded me of the way words would change during the seventies
how news bulletins would change a word even in one day reporting Ireland
how the words on something would evolve to a kind of more acceptable slant

and I told him how I used to rant on then
I laughed how I used to rant on then in the seventies and eighties
all this stuff about changing the laws for the Irish situation
how they would bring the diplock courts over here when they felt they could
how they would find another emergency over here when it suited them

I was really relaxed talking to the young man I know the story of this place
I grew up in it I have eyes and ears
I try to find out different views
it's part of being free and honest that's what I was so keen to tell him
it's not part of being a member of anything it's just part of being alive

but there was something about that mention of terror
something about the way he reacted to me talking about it
looking back it was almost as if he was suddenly on the job
and his face changed just that wee bit, his eyes caught mine just for a second

though it was only a couple of days later
when I was up for the toilet in the middle of the night
I was up for my usual four o'clock pee
and I'd decided to have a cup of tea and a banana
when it suddenly dawned on me
just out the blue

jesus christ that cunt was a cop!
that wasn't a nice young man looking for the wisdom of the old
that cunt was a cop!
it's the War on Terror! he was part of the war on terror!
and that's why his eyes changed when I spoke about that

of course you can never really be sure of these things
you can't really tell there's no way of knowing
who can you trust? can you trust anyone ever?

there seems to be so much being spent on this war on terror
so much about how we need to have more secret police
how much we need more phonetapping
all the news about threats to the fabric of our society
how the whole world is being taken over

it makes me wonder just because I keep questioning it
I can't help it it's just the way I am
I like to be free and honest
I hate language that isn't free and honest

that's just the truth of it
I can't put it any other way

and I keep opening my mouth and saying it
what else is there to do when you're growing old?
you can't go to your grave without having said what you think

I suppose they just have to keep files on people like me
if I was one of them, I imagine I would

Wish You Were Here

(1)

people
not doing whatever it is
they do
when they're not here

dressed
as to announce
together
they are not what they are
in their other place

and the glass bottomed boat
leaves from the pier
in half an hour

(2)

nobody cares if
the moors or the martians
lived here
in the thirteenth century

somebody [they say] has been here
that morsel of history

comes with the chips
and the pork chop

the young people here
for their hole
and the beer

–they have the right idea

(3)

a local mother and her child
a local man smoking a pipe
a local dog lying in the shade
a local somebody going about their work

how *authentic*

(4)

never so easy –

having pocketed
where you have been

wandering on
with semi-certainty
to show in future

the particular place
you put your stethoscope
to what it was

you had been told
was there

(5)

only the children
properly

where they are
who they are

to tourist and local
of tourist and local

and the function of the adults
to give them all their time

getting on with it

To be free of this supposed authority, the physical burden of having to relate unexpectedly to the challenge as to whether authority recognises you. Veneration of dispensers of value.

These matters can be strategic, having the other self that has been seen in a church that the person who has opted to approach you, daily frequents.

Trust in the clergy is part of the supposed given, no escape from the judgment by proxy: the clergy have told us you are a source of our value, of our society's value, the hearty We did not know you were one of us before or:

to get on with your work in peace away from this person, yourself, who is supposed to have been in church and to whom these people have now extended their welcome

food for thought

the mushroom cloud

Plasma Nights

seductive bright light
    of the evening narrative

ease of habit
    the need to relax

heck
    we all need a break

so it goes
    day into night

something to talk about
    social cohesion

* * *

which is entertainment
    which is value

which is passing time
    which is bonding

movement on the retina
    movement in the brain

reinforcement
    which is

processed information
    spectator dialogue

plasma brother

*   *   *   *

privileged
                by bombs
                we occupy

the dominant narrative
for subjects

far away
who may envy us

if seen
on their screen

The Proxy Badge of Victimhood

when the colonial oppressor
wears the proxy badge of victimhood

when the state talks about democracy
and boasts about democracy
and busses in its voters
from the 4 corners of the globe

when the possession of nationality
is a foot landing on an airport tarmac
and the dispossessed fester
in the camps of the dispossessed

---

when spokespersons for the state
are good at explaining the current position in English
because they are English
and good at sounding American
because they are American

and the natives are hopeless spokespersons
who speak in heavily accented English
because they are not English
who don't sound American
because they are not American

they are foreigners
on their native soil
and they sound like foreigners
because that's all they are
to the English, and to the Americans
and to the incoming dispossessors

foreigners

---

statehood is right to arms
statehood is control of the air

and the state walls up the natives
the state drives roads through their livelihood
the state uproots their livelihood

statehood is tank
statehood is bulldozer of homes

---

state killing is not killing
state killing is justifiable context
state killing is the operation of justice

stateless killing is simply killing
stateless killing is never context
stateless killing is motiveless evil

we are the state
you are the stateless

the battle is good versus evil
what more history do you need?

---

to accuse the state of oppression
is genocide

to accuse the state of racism
is genocide

to accuse the state of colonial expansion
is genocide

no one wants to be accused of genocide
much better to turn a blind eye

---

but the state is oppressive
but the state is racist
but the state is intent on colonial expansion

and the state colonises the past
the state says its people are the single victims of history

yet many are the victims of history
no single people has precedence

---

we inherit no victimhood from the murdered in the genocides of history
we inherit no guilt from the murderers in the genocides of history

they are the dead
we are the living

who alone are responsible for our actions
who cannot forever blame our role as victims

to be oppressive
to be racist
to be intent on colonial expansion

wearing the proxy badge of victimhood

Litany: Blair's Britain

to seek the truth
is to foment terrorism

to call war state violence
is to foment terrorism

to question the news
is to foment terrorism

to press the mute button
is to foment terrorism

to call Bush fundamentalist
is to foment terrorism

to study Blair's hand-gestures
is to foment terrorism

to shout "Down with Castlereagh"
is to foment terrorism

to think "the universal human"
is to foment terrorism

who dines with Blair?
who dines with the journalists?

to play tennis with Lord Levy
is a jolly good show

junk language surround us
junk food comfort us

American foreign policy
domestic monetarist policy

b-52
pray for us

CBU-72 cluster
pray for us

trident nuclear
jolly good show

to be free from fear
is to foment terrorism

to feel free within
is to foment terrorism

to foment fear
to foment fear
to foment fear

is Blair's Britain

Epithalamium

For Stephen and Lucy

Let me not to the marriage of true minds admit impediment
Shakespeare says – and maybe it *is* something to do with minds.
Or there again, something to do with everything else
you can think of; going to the shops, sitting in a bus together,
who you want to waken up beside in the morning,
And who you want to go to bed with – for the rest of your life.
Who you're going to have your most important rows with
who you want to share your silences, who you want to share
your money with, if you have any. Who you want to share
your poverty with, if you don't. Who you *can* share your poverty with,
and still get on when there's no fancy stuff to occupy your minds.
It's maybe being thirty with somebody, being forty with somebody,
being fifty, being sixty, getting used to ways of doing things
with the same person, getting used to *not* doing things with them
when you have to go your separate ways to raise the dough
for a house. "The trouble with marriage," I used to say,
is you have to stop *living* with each other." All this up at
the crack of dawn stuff, out to your separate jobs,
who's first home at night, who makes the dinner, if anybody
makes it. And all the account business, joint or separate. And the
usual list as to who does what, ironing, hoovering, washing
the clothes. Who does what. Who's got lousy habits. Who thinks
their farts are funny. Who's the most incomprehensible, opaque,
wrongheaded pain in the arse you could ever find, and you've
found them living with you. But give it an hour. Or a day.
And watch out for the wisecracks. There's Chekhov:
"If you can't stand loneliness don't get married" – and there's
no shortage of busted-up couples out there who won't bust
a gut with grief if you join them. You stick your own way. To
hell with them. It's not a sentimental thing, it's a serious thing
the most serious thing you'll ever do, if you're doing it properly
as you are. Saying it to others, before others, this is who I want,
this is where it ends and begins with me. And uniquely so.
So here's to you, Stephen and Lucy, standing at that old portal:
here's to a good road before you, and a long one,
and the two of you walking together happily, down it.

Being a Human Being

for Mordechai Vanunu

not to be complicit
not to accept everyone else is silent it must be alright

not to keep one's mouth shut to hold onto one's job
not to accept public language as cover and decoy

not to put friends and family before the rest of the world
not to say I am wrong when you know the government is wrong

not to be just a bought behaviour pattern
to accept the moment and fact of choice

I am a human being
and I exist

a human being
and a citizen of the world

responsible to that world
-and responsible for that world

An Ayrshire Mother

the last pey in the factory   1933
before a got married

the last thing a could sign for
before the family allowance

ma husband tommy
ma daughter cathie
eric john and tom

ma womans weekly
ma peoples friend
ma ardrossan n saltcoats herald

a four in a block   toilet n bathroom
up n doon stairs   front n back gairden

a says tay tommy   when they gave us the keys
ahl die in this hoose

lik the folk acroass the road
n the kellys next door
ah pit oot a coronation flag
an tommy no pleased

coorss tommy's frae dublin
bit ahm scottish no irish
we're maybe a catholic faimily
bit she's oor queen inaw

ma rosary beads
ma womans guild
ma chapel

the wance a week
yistirdays paper

under thir chin
bone combin

yir soacks is in the drawer
a clean shirt   ower the back a that chair

did yi wahsh yir neck

huxterin aboot
yir face in that book

look   the suns oot
get some air aboot they legs

C&A
arnott simpson's
lewis's stores

a wabbit article
loaded wi messages
back fay the toon

the ashes cowpt
nay loass
whut a freen gets

the hooss redd up
ma brasses done
the claes stepp

sheets oot the back
tatties n the boil
ahl gie the soup a steer

a new rigoot   coort shin

tom   speak proper

In Memoriam
Mary McConnon Mulgrew
(1909-78)

the sacred heart
above the winterdykes
set roon the fire

---

four in a block = type of council house; coronation flag = flag at the Queen's coronation in June 1953; bone combin = dust combing (children's heads); huxterin = lounging idly; C&A etc = former department stores; wabbit article = tired person; cowpt = emptied out; redd up = tidied up; claes stepp = clothes steeped; a steer = a stir; rigoot = rigout, set of clothes, attire; coort shin = court shoes; the sacred heart = an image of Christ often seen in the living room of Catholic homes; winterdykes = folding clothes horse (historical, in summer clothes hung over rural dykes outside).

that each
one be the
subject of
their own
narration

as to
become
verb

Three Types of Envoi

(1)

Odysseus

it took me so long to get back to who I am

why was I away so long   why was the journey so tortuous

all those false masks against a backdrop narrative to do with authenticity

but now arriving back there is still much debris to clear

the clearer to see the point from which I started

that from which I set out confused in sundry identities at war with themselves

now to find calm on that setting-out point as the final destination

(2)

A humanist

The son of an immigrant, he had eschewed the culture of his father as also that of the land into which he was born.

The religion of his father was once the religion of the indigenous natives, but they had rejected and overthrown it.

And the son was yet seen as of that tribe which corroded the native culture and language.

An outsider, he felt at home with the art and culture of other outsiders, for many years he found companionship across space and time.

But from within he came to realise himself as instance of the universal human. The universal human is inclusive and absolute, there is no individual outside it.

This sense of the universal human is the home of all those who have won through to become themselves.

And much trouble in the world is caused by those who remain self-sequestered in their perceived province of the exclusive.

(3)

A life

There were some who seemed to spend their lives "being a writer".
And he had spent his life not being a writer.
That way lay safety. An invisibility. A freedom.

Those he met saw him as "that writer" and would never understand that this was not how he had chosen to see himself.
He accepted their seeing him as "that writer" almost with a kind of irony.

But then he began to accept that he was a writer.
It was a matter of language and consciousness. The link between the two.

He had to choose to accept the responsibility of the outer that he had preserved from himself, that he had left to the perception of others.

For as he grew older he stood in a separate relationship to himself.
He was able to body himself conceptually as a totality.

And though he had never been a storyteller, he saw that he had been telling a story all his life.
It became important to him that somebody heard the story, now that he realised he had been telling it.

Yet all that remained to be told was that he had been telling it.
And all that remained was the need for the last understanding, the sign that someone had heard the story, and the teller was no longer necessary.